I BELIEVE—
AND WHY

by

R. R. WILLIAMS

Bishop of Leicester

LONDON

A. R. MOWBRAY & CO LTD

©   *A. R. Mowbray & Co. Ltd.* 1970

*Printed in Great Britain at the
Pitman Press, Bath*

SBN: 264 64546 4

First published in 1971

OTHER BOOKS BY THE SAME AUTHOR:

Authority in the Apostolic Age (S.C.M.)

Commentaries:

Acts (S.C.M.)
Letters of John and James (C.U.P.)

What's Right with the Church of England (*Lutterworth*)

230
w675

Contents

Foreword

WE ARE told in the Pastoral Epistles to 'fight the good fight of faith'. In our day, this challenge has ceased to be a formality or a convention. It is a fight to win faith; a fight to hold faith; a fight to spread faith. But the fight is still 'a good fight', a fight maintained by good hope, capable of being supported by good arguments, and of being rewarded by good and lasting possessions.

This book is written in the hope that it may help some of its readers to go on fighting this good fight. It reveals at times that its writer, like many of its readers, knows the problems as well as the promises of believing faith in the modern world. Like many who dare to say 'I believe', he has to add at once 'help thou my unbelief'.

The second chapter (a short 'essay on man') is based on a lecture given at Christ Church, Northampton, in Lent 1970.

It remains for me only to express my thanks to my secretary, Mrs. Audrey Gibbons, for her ready help in typing the manuscript, and to Canon Purcell for encouraging me to accept the responsibility of writing it.

June 1970   RONALD LEICESTER

GOD

'To A discerning eye', wrote W. R. Matthews (afterwards Dean of St. Paul's) in 1930, 'it must be clear that
the main question which is being decided in the world
today is whether or not the majority of men shall continue to believe in God'.[1] To Christians, vaguely or consciously troubled by the increasingly vociferous nature of
contemporary unbelief, whether of the atheistic or agnostic
type, it may be comforting to think that such was the
situation forty years ago. They may feel with some relief
that if things were like that then, it is surprising that they
are not even worse today than they seem to be. Social
surveys reveal that a high percentage of English people
believe, or say they believe, in God. It is however fair to
wonder what kind of a God they believe in, and how far
the faith they claim to have is anything more than a
vestigial relic of what all Englishmen once believed, and
whether it is a faith that could stand up to any serious
challenge or enquiry.

Whatever may be the answer to those questions, there
can be no doubt that 'belief in God' (whatever exact content is to be given to those words) is absolutely basic to
Christian religion. This faith stands fairly and squarely at
the beginning of the Creeds—'I believe in God the
Father Almighty, Maker of heaven and earth' in the
Apostles' Creed, and 'I believe in One God the Father

[1] *God in Christian Thought and Experience*, Nisbet, p. xi.

Almighty, Maker of heaven and earth, and of all things visible and invisible' in the Nicene Creed. It is briefly and succinctly expressed in the summary in the old Catechism, 'I learn to believe in God the Father, who made me and all the world'. It is impossible to make sense of the rest of the Creed if we skip or fudge this fundamental clause at its start. The same thing applies in a different way to the Bible. 'In the beginning God' is its sublime opening. The whole story of the Old Testament is the story of God's dealings with one people, the Hebrews, with passing glances at his dealings with the surrounding nations as well. God is clearly presented as the 'maker of heaven and earth', not only in Genesis but also in the Psalms and in Isaiah.

The New Testament is the story of how Jesus of Nazareth came to be equated, or at least 'bracketed' with God. His unique contribution was to live a life of peculiarly close filial trust in God as his Father, and in obedience to him, although this life was in a unique degree lived for men, for others. There is some anticipation, perhaps more than anticipation, of that differentiation in Divine functions that led before long to the formulation of the so-called 'Doctrine of the Trinity'. What is inconceivable is to read the Bible intelligently with 'belief in God' subtracted from it. The most radical 'Christian atheists' would admit that their atheism finds no place in the Bible except in the mouths of fools ('The fool hath said in his heart: There is no God.' Psalm 53. 1).

It is natural to find the same assumption running right through the Prayer Book and all the Church's worship. Every prayer, every psalm, every hymn assumes the existence and the personal nature of God, accessible to human hopes, aspirations and desires, ever more ready to hear than we to pray.

None of this in itself 'proves' the existence of God. It all might be one vast delusion. We used to sing

> The heathen in his blindness
> Bows down to wood and stone.

It is conceivably possible that the Christian might be the victim of similar delusion, and that the unseen Being to whom their prayers are offered might be no more able to hear and answer than the idols of other centuries and other lands. 'Ears have they and hear not'—but what if the Christians' God is as deaf and dumb as all the rest? Once the question is asked, 'Do I, can I, believe in God?' there is no stopping the enquiry until the ultimate questions have been boldly faced. We may find indeed that they cannot be satisfactorily answered in the language in which they are asked. We may find that we shall have to live 'by faith' and not 'by sight'. We may find that God has his own ways of evoking and maintaining faith in him. But if our only defence, to ourselves and others, lies in shelving or shunning the question itself, there will always be a gnawing doubt at the back of our minds, always a skeleton lurking in our religious cupboard.

It is, of course, true that in recent years some writers, especially in America, have embarked on the perilous course of trying to produce a kind of atheism that is compatible with a kind of Christianity. They link up closely with the so-called 'Death of God' theologians, although there are so many variations of viewpoint among the latter that not all of them can be classed in the 'Christian atheist' group. Christian atheists, scared of making any metaphysical assertions, and sometimes influenced by provocative statements of Dietrich Bonhoeffer to the effect that we have to live before God as though he did not exist, have tried to extract from the Christian tradition such

3

relics of its insights into human behaviour as in their view could survive 'the death of God'. Their attitude is like an extreme form of the view (commonly held in the nineteenth century) that Christian morals could survive without the support of Christian doctrine or dogma. Although it is true that morals have their own autonomy, the results of the divorce so far available do not seem encouraging. The permissive society and the crime wave have followed hard on the heels of a non-dogmatic faith. Perhaps they need not have done, but in fact they have. There is not much future for Christian atheism: perhaps Christianity will survive, perhaps atheism. Perhaps both can survive side by side, but they cannot coalesce and survive in a mutual embrace.

Now I am anxious in this book to face real difficulties and not to dodge them so I want to ask myself (and my readers by implication) what are the real difficulties about belief in God? I believe they arise from the atmosphere in which all of us have to live, whether we like it or not. 'God' is not an observable, audible, or tangible object similar to other objects of whose existence we are vividly, or at least tacitly aware. If we are to believe in God it must be either because the world of objects that we know compels us to postulate his existence in order to retain a sane and coherent attitude to life, or because he has his own way of making us aware of him, quite apart from any direct contact with any of our 'senses'—our sight, hearing, taste or smell. We may find that both approaches—we might call them roughly the rational and the religious—have a contribution to make to our 'sense of the presence of God'.

The atmosphere in which we live is certainly (or at least superficially) hostile to belief in God, and this whether we think of the scientific, the technological, the philosophical or the theological environments that surround us.

The scientific atmosphere (and I think more of the popular atmosphere prevailing in a scientific world than of the attitudes of leading scientists as such) is an atmosphere which is scornful of the 'science' of the Bible, and hardly realises that Christians do not feel themselves any more bound by this than do the scientists themselves. It has hardly yet woken up to the fact that Christians read Genesis 1–3 as sublime poetry and not as in any sense literally true, though they find in such chapters many insights of permanent spiritual value. The popular scientific atmosphere is an atmosphere of cosmic law, in which there is no room for miracles. The universal validity of mathematical calculation, and the steady progress of medicine based on proved bio-chemical discoveries predispose modern man to reject out of hand miracles up to now firmly embedded in Christian tradition, and miracles which might yet be expected. The popular scientific atmosphere is an atmosphere in which it is hard to believe that human beings are of special interest to, or capable of having any relations with, the Ultimate Power behind the universe, if such Ultimate Power there be. The sheer vastness of the universe, whether measured in space or in time, easily makes men dubious of any statements concerning man dating from pre-Copernican times.

The technological atmosphere, though closely related to the scientific, is in some respects distinguishable from it. It concerns the use made of science in daily life. In some ways it adds no problems of an ultimate character to those which arose when man first made fire, cooked his food, or used a wheel. But 'the rate of change of the rate of change' *seems* to have made a difference. It is difficult, for instance, to estimate just what difference to man's religious thoughts the journeys to the moon have made. It so happens that the journeys were made by religious men,

5

and the impact on religious opinion was less revolutionary than it might have been if such had not been the case. To hear Genesis read from the space-ship was at least superficially more helpful than hearing, shall we say, a piece from Bertrand Russell. But only superficially. The *deep* impression surely was that man was infinitely cleverer than he had thought himself to be. If he could do this, what couldn't he do, given time and opportunity? The moon of the Bible and the moon of the poets were eclipsed together by the moon of technological man. At least one of the great 'works of God',

> the silver moon by night
> Midst her spangled sisters bright

had been domesticated, conquered, de-sacralised.

The philosophical atmosphere is not helpful to belief in God. The middle years of this century have seen a great advance in what is called analytical or linguistic philosophy. This school of thought has diverted the interest of philosophers from 'what is', 'what is the case', to the study of statements and their logical significance. According to this school, the only statements that have any meaning are those that can be verified, and the only verification usually in mind is verification through the senses. To this school, therefore, statements about the existence of God are not so much false as meaningless. For many centuries Christian belief in God could look to the great thinkers of the past, to Plato and Aristotle in particular, for thoughts which were at least compatible with Christian thoughts about the *summum bonum* or the Creator of the Universe. Now such thoughts are not so much denied as ridiculed as meaningless. The Christian believer finds himself isolated from more and more of his contemporaries who in earlier times would have been his allies. Our age is not likely to

6

produce men like St. Thomas, Richard Hooker, A. E. Taylor or William Temple. The tree on which such fruit grew has itself been cut down.

Even the theological atmosphere is harsh and cold. Biblical criticism has altered the status of the raw material on which much theological enquiry was previously based. The New English Bible version of the Old Testament has made obvious to ordinary readers what scholars have long known. The Old Testament 'anticipations' of Christ are much less obvious in the original, for instance, than they appeared to be in the Authorised Version, with its 'Christian' headings (for instance 'The mutual love of Christ and his Church'[1]), its capital 'S' for Spirit of God, and its many turns of expression which seemed to prepare the way for the coming of Christ. The great emphasis on *fulfilment* as found in St. Matthew and St. John is seen to raise more questions than it solves. The critical study of the Gospels has gone much further than most church people realise. The element of 'interpretation', which many have come to accept in connection with the Fourth Gospel, is known to play a big part in the other Gospels as well. It is not necessary to accept the extreme radicalism of Rudolf Bultmann to find onself reading the Gospels in a way quite different from that to which centuries of our forebears in the faith have read them. Meanwhile questions of a dogmatic kind are more openly canvassed. The Virgin Birth and the Empty Tomb are publicly denied as they have been long questioned by men of repute in the church. All dogmatic statements based on the Fourth Gospel (and there are many) have to be re-examined in the light of modern views on that Gospel. Many have tried to adjust their 'image of God' in the light of Dr. John Robinson's slogan 'Our image of God

[1] The Song of Solomon, chapter 2.

7

must go'. Some of them have lost their old image well enough, but not found another to take its place. So it is that among Christians, as well as among the uncommitted, many whose faith in God had seemed secure and steadfast now find themselves assailed by doubt. They kneel to pray, but find themselves saying 'I wonder if there is anyone to hear'.

In this situation we turn back to 'arguments for the existence of God'. Most clergymen have not thought about them since an early stage in their study of Christian doctrine, when probably they could reel off four or five classical arguments, without feeling that they played any vital part in their own faith. In modern books the classical arguments are for the most part treated as having nothing worthwhile to contribute to faith in a Living God. It is said truly enough that the God who arrives on the scene only as the last stage in an abstract argument, or as an inference from nature, from literature, or from conscience is not the God of the Bible or of recognisable Christian faith. But the classical arguments (or improved and modernised forms of them) may still have a real, if limited part to play. These are times, as we have said, of doubt and perplexity. There is a question which can easily arise even in devout minds—the question whether the God of faith, the God of prayer, the God of personal or corporate religious experience stands in any definite relationship to the God (if such there be) of Creation. Browning posed the question as to whether the Almighty were 'the All-loving too': today the question is whether the All-loving is the Almighty too. At such moments it may be helpful to have considered, calmly and rationally, the evidence, if there is any, for 'the existence of God'. It may be helpful to have asked oneself whether the atheist's interpretation of the universe is the only one to which the

8

evidence points, or whether, even on the scientist's terms, other views are not possible, or even probable.

The Creeds begin with a confession that God is the Maker of all things. This is a positive assertion of the faith to which the so-called cosmological argument was thought to point. Following Aristotle, who taught that all moving things owed their motion to an 'Unmoved Mover', St. Thomas taught that all finite, temporal things depended for their existence on an infinite, eternal source or cause. This is a sophisticated way of expressing the common-sense view of the ordinary man who assumes that every-thing *must* have a maker: if he looks at a box or a cricket bat he assumes that it could not have made itself. In the same way he looks at the earth, the sea, the sky and draws the same conclusion. This may seem very naïve, very crude, but it conceals a deep and ineluctable truth. It is abundantly clear that no scientific enquiry takes us any nearer than we were before to knowing how 'the earth and the worlds were made'. Scientists may discuss things like spontaneous explosion of hydrogen gases but this only leads to the question 'how did the hydrogen gas get there?' Our questions are something like those of the four-year-old who keeps saying to his mother 'why this?' and 'why that?' until he reaches a point at which mother is either too tired, too busy, or too discreet to be able to answer any more. However far we go back or however far we go 'out' (for we need not assume that creation is necessarily a past event) we can only think of still more distant time, or still more extensive space. Even when we think, as Christians do, of past eternities, 'before the world was', it is virtually impossible to think otherwise than of further past time, though possibly not measured in centuries or millenia. One thing is quite certain, and perhaps it is necessary to make the point, and that is that nothing that

9

science can discover about the structure of matter or the past history of the stars, can throw any light, one way or the other, on the critical question as to whether the universe stands, or does not stand, in relation to a Creative Mind on which all else depends.

The other argument which deserves mention, even in a brief book, is what is called the teleological argument. This means the argument from 'ends'—from the *apparent* fact that existent realities, from the unmeasurably small to the overwhelmingly great, are so designed as to fulfil a function for which they are evidently suited—the eye for seeing, the ear for hearing, the sun for shining, and so on. The discovery of evolution may seem to support this argument rather than undermine it, although the theory of natural selection can also be so interpreted as to make the existence of a Divine Planner less rather than more necessary. It is impossible to go deeply into this vast subject, but to put the problem very crudely there is always the question whether the eye is designed for seeing or whether organisms with things like eyes happen to see, and therefore survive. A man, however, who still thinks there 'is something in' the teleological argument is not therefore to be classed a fool. Teilhard de Chardin has shown us that it is possible to be a reputable scientist and an outstanding philosopher and theologian and to hold a teleological view with renewed force and vigour.

If we are anxious to find an 'argument' that has real and indisputable force (not of course such force as to end all argument) we shall turn to the argument from personality. The flowers turning towards the sun may seem to show to us that rudimentary response to environment which may prefigure more active and spontaneous responses at 'higher' levels of creation. We do not know exactly what consciousness means to animals (though we may be sure they have some). But we are sure that we are conscious, that the stream of sensations, thoughts and emotions in the midst of which each of us lives is something 'very special' in the context of the created world—possibly and probably unique. As William Temple once said 'When I look at the stars I know that they are there. The stars do not know that I am here.' He argued from that that the sheer *size* of the universe was no cause for believing that man's personality was not of special importance in the scheme of things. No one knows what may be discovered tomorrow—we may find other worlds than this with equivalent or even higher forms of personality than those we know, but it is at least interesting that *so far* no other part of the solar system has been discovered in which life at all like our own would be possible. If a man likes to believe that man is not an accidental development on one tiny planet, and that the conditions of that planet are intended to make possible the high and complex pheno- menon known as man, no scientist can prove him a fool or an idiot. 'By faith we understand that the worlds have been framed by the word of God so that what is seen hath not been made out of things which do appear' (Hebrews 11. 3). If a man has this 'faith' it cannot be taken away by the things of 'sight'. Faith is the very function of man's soul by which he penetrates into the unseen and the unknown.

The man who believes that the whole created process is literally a chance happening, an accident, seems to me to show a credulity by the side of which Christian belief looks like hard-headed rationalism. As Edward Conklin writes 'The probability of life originating from accident is comparable to the probability of a dictionary resulting from an explosion in a printing works' (quoted by Michael Green, *Runaway World*, I.V.P., 1968, p. 55). If for dictionary' one writes the plays of Shakespeare, the music of Beethoven, the invention of radar, the love of families and friends, one begins to get the scale of the credulity required.

And the 'argument from personality' is not confined to the argument from the existence of persons, such as each person knows himself to be, but includes that infinitely varied world of relationships between persons which for most people provides the most enriching element in their human existence. Life seems to tell us that the making and the expressing of our personality is quite the most significant element in our experience, but that this would be virtually non-existent but for our relationships with other persons. So when we hope, or when we believe, that there is 'something personal' at the heart of things we are not suggesting that God is just another Person like ourselves. All we are saying is that we cannot contemplate an inanimate system producing anything so infinitely rich and varied as a world of persons if the source of all things was 'less than Personal'. It is perhaps significant that without any formal understanding of personal relationships as modern psychology has revealed them, the early Church arrived at an understanding of God's Nature as not monolithically isolated, but as inclusive of mutuality, one of the principal corollaries of the doctrine of the Holy Trinity.

Christians have sometimes been tempted to see the work of God only in those aspects of the world that at any one time defy explanation. This leads to what is called 'a God of the gaps' and this is rightly rejected. God must be the Creator and sustainer of all, or he is nothing. The real error is not the believing in a God of the gaps (for God is the maker of all things, visible and invisible, revealed and unrevealed) but loss of faith in the God of the filled-in gaps—as though the fact that we know a little more about *how* things work tells us *why* things work, and how they come to be there, and to work like that.

Before we turn, in conclusion, to faith in God as itself a gift of God, we must just glance at a difficulty of quite another kind. Granted that a case can be made for the existence of some kind of a 'Being' behind all 'Becoming', does not the nature of the world point to a Being at best supremely indifferent to human values, or even hostile to them? This is the problem of evil. Certainly there is no reason to consider the problem of evil in isolation from the problem of good, but as what we profess is belief in God *the Father*, i.e. a God of love, it is the problem of *evil* that causes the stumbling block. There is no easy answer to this great problem, as the unsuccessful efforts of all Job's comforters amply testify. Only one brief thought can be offered at this point and it is this. Christians find in the Cross of Christ the supreme moment of revelation; to them it is the most fully significant of all human events. If such a moment of horror, suffering and sin has proved to Christians generations such a vehicle of divine humility and love that in it is seen God's true glory, perhaps there is nothing so bad that through it, in it, or in spite of it, God's love cannot shine through. This seems to me a better approach than that of the so-called 'process theologians'. These are the Christian thinkers who have built upon A. N. Whitehead's philosophical system (where stress is laid on the importance of the *sequence* of events, rather than what remains unchanged while time rolls on). Some of us have so accustomed ourselves to Plato's view that 'time is the moving image of eternity' (cf. Ellerton's hymn—

O strength and stay, upholding all creation
Who ever dost thyself unchanged abide)

13

that we shall never easily absorb a picture of the Deity as himself caught up in the stream of changing events. We may nevertheless admit that the 'process' approach may do justice to certain aspects of Christian doctrine, especially to God's involvement in human history, better than the static image of the 'Unmoved Mover' that has influenced successive generations of Christian thinkers even if they have never heard the phrase.

We may then, in our preliminary thinking about 'whether there is a God', or in our moments of doubt and depression, derive some limited help from those arguments to which thoughtful Christians have given weight in centuries past. But no one will expect true, personal faith to depend on such arguments. This has other sources. What are they?

St. Paul (or whoever wrote Ephesians) said that faith is not 'of ourselves'—we cannot stir it up or create it—'it is the gift of God'. This chimes in with what the great saints have said and thought, and with the experience that we have ourselves shared. 'Thou wouldest not be seeking me if thou hadst not already found me' was the word Pascal heard from God, and to have found God in this sense means to have been found by him. St. Augustine, and endless other saints of God, have testified to their belief that God was seeking them long before they were seeking him. Mature modern Christians, like the late John Baillie, have repeatedly stated that they could never remember the time when they were not aware of being surrounded by an environment which to them was a Personal Being, pervasive, demanding and loving. Many explanations of this can be given—it could be a projection from the childish mind made in imitation of parental attitudes; it could be a projection into the unseen of the parents who themselves were 'all around' the child as he first emerged to consciousness. Equally it is possible that this was God's way of making the child aware from the beginning of his life of his gracious presence. If God gives air and milk and sleep, and whatever else the child needs, is it so great a thing if he lets the light of his countenance begin to shine upon the soul?

In any case, the Christian who says 'I believe in God'—meaning by that not 'I consent to the probable existence of a personal God' but 'I throw myself in trust upon my faithful Creator'—does so in response to initiatives from outside himself.

These may come from the Bible, either from what is read there, or from the tradition which has been fostered by the Bible as read and preached in the church. Anyone who, for instance, has read or sung the Psalms from his youth has learned a language of communication with God —words to use in speech to God, words to hear as God's voice to him. This is a real medium of revelation. 'The goodly fellowship of the prophets' and 'the glorious company of the apostles'—if their words are known and heeded, give endless testimony to the reality of the Living God. Most clearly of all, Jesus of Nazareth, to Christians the Lord Christ, makes the Father known. He takes us by the hand, and teaches us to say 'Our Father', as he himself said 'Abba—Father' with such unforgettable trust and love that his followers remembered and preserved the very Aramaic word, even when the language of the church had changed to Greek.

Always we must distinguish between knowing about God and knowing him. Christian faith is not holding right views about God: it is living in a certain relationship with him. If we would know him better we must trust him more fully and obey him more completely. There is no other way. We must catch (from Our Lord himself, or from our contemporaries whom he can use) the confidence that he *is* there, that he is here, that he can be trusted and that if we try to obey him he will help our weaknesses and reward our faith. 'He that cometh to God must believe that *he is*, and that he is the rewarder of those that diligently seek him.' (Hebrews 11. 6).

Faith stands in contrast to unbelief, to credulity, and to 'sight'. There will always be an element of *venture* in it. 'Hope that is seen is not hope.' If we could see and prove all, there would be no place left for faith. But if we desire faith, if we long for God, if we want to obey him, 'we shall know of the doctrine'. We can always say, 'Lord I believe, help thou my unbelief.'

Dr. John Whale, in his splendid Cambridge lectures on Christian Doctrine, reminds us of a striking incident from the Journal of George Fox. Fox records that in 1648 in Nottinghamshire the following incidnet took place. 'One morning as I was sitting by the fire a great cloud came over me and a temptation beset me; but I sate still. And it was said: "All things come by nature"; and the elements and stars came over me, so that I was in a manner quite clouded with it . . . . And as I sate still under it, and let it alone, a living hope arose in me, and a true voice which said "There is a living God who made all things". And immediately the cloud and temptation vanished away and life rose over it all; my heart was glad and I praised the living God. After some time I met with some people who had such a notion that there was no God, but that all things come by nature. I had a great dispute with them and made some of them confess that there is a living God. Then I saw that it was good that I had gone through that exercise.'

2

MAN

'WHAT A piece of work is a man! How noble in reason!
How infinite in faculty! in form and moving how express
and admirable! in action how like an angel! in apprehen-
sion how like a god! the beauty of the world! the paragon
of animals! And yet to me, what is this quintessence of
dust? man delights not me, nor woman neither.' Paragon
of animals—quintessence of dust: so Hamlet, but of
course really Shakespeare, writing in 1602.

> Know then thyself, presume not God to scan
> The proper study of mankind is man.
> Placed in this isthmus of a middle state
> A being darkly wise, and rudely great: . . .
> Created half to rise, and half to fall;
> Great Lord of all things, yet a prey to all;
> Sole judge of truth, in endless error hurled;
> The glory, jest and riddle of the world.

So Alexander Pope, in his *Essay on Man*, in 1733.

> Where is one that, born of woman, altogether can escape
> From the lower world within him, moods of tiger, or of ape?
> Man as yet is being made, and ere the crowning Age of Ages,
> Shall not aeon after aeon pass and touch him into shape?
> All about him shadow still, but while the races flower and
>   fade,
> Prophet eyes may catch a glory slowly gaining on the shade,
> Till the peoples all are one, and all their voices blend in
>   choric
> Hallelujah to the Maker, 'It is finished. Man is made'.

That was Tennyson, writing after Darwin's *Origin of Species* had revolutionised, or could we say 'evolutionised' man's understanding of himself, his past and his future.

Now let us go back to more familiar territory, to the Bible, and to its whole picture of man and his place in God's purposes. The key passage is Psalm 8, especially verse 4, 'Lord, what is man, that thou visitest him, or the son of man that thou regardest him?' This psalm sees man as occupying a special place in God's creation. Externally, spatially, he is nothing compared with the heavens, the sun, moon and stars. But because of God's special relationship with him, he is only a little lower than the angels, crowned with glory and honour, made to have dominion over the works of God's hands, and to have all things in subjection under his feet—sheep, oxen, the beasts of the field; fowls of the air and fishes of the sea and whatever 'walketh through the paths of the seas'. This brings out both sides of man's nature—his physical littleness and his teleological greatness.

The stories of Genesis bring out other aspects of the biblical doctrine of man. The stories, though not historical, portray permanent truths of great value. Man is formed out of the dust—physically he is part of the space–time continuum, but he is made in the image of God. He is made for fellowship with God, given great but limited scope and authority. But he fails to keep his station, and after the fall is ill-at-ease in matters of sex—he has to wear fig leaves; in his relations with the animal world—the serpent bruises his heel; and with his own race—Cain slays Abel. Paradise is lost, and the rest of the Bible tells the long story of how costly it was for it to be regained.

> O generous love, that He, Who smote
> In Man, for man the foe,

The double agony in Man
For man, should undergo.

Newman had seen the importance of St. Paul's teaching on the first Adam and the last Adam (called by Newman the *second* Adam). 'As in Adam all die, even so in Christ shall all be made alive.' All men share in Adam's sin and weakness, not really by infection or hereditary taint—it is just an empirical fact to be observed, that all men sin. But all men retain something of the infinite possibilities that God had in mind for them: all can be saved and redeemed through union with Christ, 'the proper man'.

It may be helpful at this point to desert literary and biblical statements, and to take a cool look at man as we actually find him today, using our own powers of scientific observation, such as they are, to help us in our task.

First we notice that man is an animal. The *Oxford Dictionary* defines 'animal' as an organised being endowed (more or less perceptibly) with life, sensations, and voluntary motion! Man clearly qualifies under this definition. An observer from another planet, arriving over the earth by air, would not immediately differentiate the animal 'man' from the animal 'ape' except that he would notice that in some parts of the world some of the former animals insulate their bodies from the cold by the use of clothes, and shield their forms from the eyes of the prurient by the same method. Food, sleep, methods of reproduction, growth from infancy to old age, from birth to death, are markedly similar. Consciousness we know to be a feature of our own form of animal existence; we cannot speak with precision about the consciousness of other animals. We know that they have some: we probably imagine that they have more than they actually do, by reading over into their minds and actions motives that we are familiar with in considering our own.

I have sometimes in confirmation addresses drawn the attention of young people, particularly in the country, to the fact that while sheep and cattle look down to the ground, men stand upright, so that they can look up to God in prayer and worship. The argument is very much *ad hominem* if not *ad infantem*, but I was pleased to come across it the other day in Calvin's Institutes, who quotes it from Ovid. This translation is by Dryden.

> While the mute creation downward bend
> Their sight, and to their earthly mother tend,
> Man looks aloft, and with erected eyes,
> Behold his own hereditary skies.
>
> (Ovid, Metam. Bk. 50)

But man is undoubtedly an animal. He is, however, a tool-making, tool-using animal. This arises from the development of his brain. He has learned to use fire, and with fire a whole series of technological instruments from the simple wheel to radar and the space-ship. It is a question whether the rapid advance of man's technological achievements in recent times does not so add to his powers and functions that it radically affects his nature. Ape— primeval peasant—moon-explorer: which gap is greater— that between ape and peasant, or that between peasant and moon-explorer? I do not know.

Man is a games-playing animal. Unlike most of the animal world his games are not confined to his childhood (lambs gambol, kittens chase cotton reels) but are continued into adult life, and cover both physical sports and pastimes, like cricket and football, and also intellectual amusements, like bridge or crossword puzzles. I do not attach much importance to all this, but perhaps it is a sophisticated way of preserving, as far as possible, the simple pleasures and excitements of early years, a means of distracting attention from the arduous concerns of adult life, whether physical or mental.

Man is a being with long-term family interests. This is indeed one of the chief differences between man and the so-called lower animals. In most levels of animal life the father's interest is confined to the moment of copulation, although there are exceptions such as are shown by bird-fathers collecting food for hen and chicks. The mother's concern is usually more prolonged, but the continuing family, involving parents, children, grand-children, aunts, and uncles, is a monopoly of human life. It is perhaps one of the ways in which the divine image survives, even in fallen man. He is what he is because he lives his whole life in close relationship with others.

He is by nature, as Aristotle said, a political animal. Aristotle treats 'the city', the political unit, as prior to the individual. 'He that is incapable of society or so complete in himself as not to want it, makes no part of a city, like a beast or a god. There is then in all persons a natural impetus to associate with each other in this manner, and he who first founded civil society was the cause of the greatest good; for as by the completion of it man is the most excellent of living beings, so without law and justice he would be the worst of all' (*Politics*, ch. 2)—words which are as true today as they were when written in 340 B.C.

Can we go further and say that man is a religious animal? Burke said so in his *Reflections on the French Revolution*—'man is by constitution a religious animal'. Some have seen the dawn of religion in the ritual bowings to the moon of some of the higher baboons. Whether or not there is anything in that, it is clear that in almost all ages, and in almost all lands, men have felt themselves in some kind of relationship with supernatural powers, and have sought, by sacrifice, by worship, by conformity to what were thought to be their wishes, to obtain their favour, and not to lose their goodwill. It is the lasting insight of the Hebrew tradition, that all such powers should rightly be comprehended in one ('the Lord our God is *one* Lord') and that fellowship with him depends at least as much on moral behaviour and social obligation as on ritual or devotional observance. St. Augustine summed it up, and gave preachers a tag for fifteen hundred years when he said, 'O God, Thou hast created us for Thyself and our heart is restless until it rest in Thee.'

So far, I think, we can go on the basis of reasonable observation and thoughtful reflection on nature and history. It is useful so to observe, and so to reflect, but I cannot claim that such observations take us very far.

So we move on to consider some of the topical issues in the conception of man—problems, tasks, opportunities, which fall upon us in a way they have not fallen upon our forefathers. These may direct us to those aspects of man's nature to which we ought to be giving attention in this changing world.

1. There is a new interest in the dignity of man as man— not as white man, educated man, rich man, governing man, but just as man. The enormous response to the cause known as *Shelter* is an example of this. There is a new sense that all need reasonable homes—rich man, poor man, beggar man, thief. 'A man's a man for a' that'. This was the fundamental idea behind the protests at the American action in Vietnam, at the sale of arms to the Federal Government in Nigeria, at the still outstanding disadvantages under which coloured people suffer in America, and even here. Whatever superficialities there may be in the judgements, however many 'lewd fellows of the baser

sort' jump on the contemporary band wagons, there is something right and true in the conception that all men are alike entitled to the basic opportunities that make human life worth its name.

2. It is this that partly lies behind the appointment of an officer at the World Council of Churches at Geneva to co-ordinate the Churches' study of man, called there, *Humanum* studies. Canon David Jenkins, a brilliant Oxford theologian, and still a Canon Theologian in my diocese, has gone to Geneva to do this work. I once asked him whether the word *humanum* was a noun or an adjective. He told me that it is really a German use of a Latin word first coined by Emil Brunner *Das Humanum*—the human being, the human idea, what makes a man—for all that! So Canon Jenkins hopes to help the Churches discover the basic, distinguishing quality of life that is truly *human*. He enlarges thus on what it is all about. 'The possibilities and necessities of planning, the uses and abuses of technological developments, the choices to be made in the application of new medical and surgical techniques, the questions raised by discoveries in genetics are all examples of factors in, and features of, our living today which force the practitioners of any and all the disciplines and professions to face this question of man, this need to consider what we are doing *to* man, and *for* man as well as simply asking what we are doing, or failing to do, *as* man is raised by the sheer pressures and possibilities of the situation, regardless of questions of faith and commitment. At the same time of course (I still quote) the developments, the pressures, and the questions bear very pointedly and heavily on traditional faiths and commitments. Thus just as the question of man is sharply and urgently posed, so the old, taken-for-granted answers to

this question are apparently finally exposed as not so much incredible as irrelevant and unhelpful. There is an immensely urgent need for guidance, sustenance and encouragement in facing the question of what men can, should and must do in order to promote human development and fulfilment.'

3. There are those who see man confronted with a startling new stage in his own evolution. Sir Julian Huxley in his essay *The Future of Man* (Churchill Ltd., 1963 and 1967) sets the stage by saying that the evolution of this planet has gone on for 5,000 million years, that life has gone on for 2,750 million years, and will continue for a similar span. His point is however that the long evolutionary process divides into three stages: the inorganic, the organic, and now the psychosocial. He claims that the evolutionary process has become self-conscious. Its results are to be seen in new cultures, philosophies, legal codes and social systems. Planning, on the widest scale, will make possible enormous leaps forward in the development of new societies, with new possibilities for all the individuals who make them up. This sounds very romantic, but is it more so than is St. Paul when he looks to see all things summed up in Christ, or Teilhard de Chardin, when he is looking forward to his Omega-point? In all wise and constructive planning, the Christian and the Church ought to have something useful to say. Christ knew what was in man, and surely we have learned something from him.

4. A feature of quite recent thinking about man is revealed in the new studies of man in his living i.e. his ecological environment. The Church Assembly recently had before it a report by the Board for Social Responsibility on *Man in his Living Environment*. This fitted in with

24

European Conservation Year, 1970, which was of course only the beginning of a long campaign and not an isolated effort. We are coming to see that even *man* must not make too much a pig of himself if he, *and* his environment, are to survive much longer. One hundred and fifty acres of forest land are cut down to make the paper for *one* edition of *one* Sunday newspaper. Great rivers and lakes are becoming poisonous sewers. The world population is growing so fast that only a miracle more staggering than the feeding of the 5,000 will prevent it starving. Man must ask in a new sense, 'What must I do to be saved?' The Churches must help man to find his way in a baffling world of change. If man is too greedy, too selfish in his exploitation of his environment, he may deprive himself of those sources of life and inward refreshment without which he cannot survive as man.

There is one more thing to say. It is right, proper, and necessary for Christians and Churches to take an occasional long, cool look at society, the world, the universe. Everything we do affects the whole. No man is an island. But most of us, most of the time, are faced with smaller questions. Each reader of this book is a man, a woman. In our own lives we have the one supreme opportunity to discover for ourselves, and hence for others, what it is to be born, to live, to die as a man—or, of course, a woman. Theologically, it is much the same! Each one of us is passing through the vale of soul-making. Where shall we seek for succour? Perhaps in a very ordinary place—in the old, unrevised Catechism. There we are taught to believe in God the Father, who made the world: in God the Son who redeemed us and all mankind: and in the Holy Spirit, who is engaged in the difficult task of sanctifying us, and all the chosen people of God. We may not have much to contribute to the salvation of man as man, but if we allow Christ to save us, we shall have done the one thing needful. At the font it was prayed for us that the old Adam might be so buried that the new man might be raised up in us. This 'new man' is of course still 'myself', but it is 'myself in Christ', who is himself, *par excellence, the* New Man. His Body is integrally one with him, and by our Baptism we are made one with him, linked to, incorporated in him, the New Man. He, Christ, the Word of the Father, is the One in whom, for whom all things consist. Christ is the key to the meaning of the Universe, and he dwells in us and we in him. Our daily task, our daily joy, is to live in the world which is made in him, and so to respond to his Spirit, in whom by Confirmation we have our share, that we daily grow up into him, unto the fullness of the measure of the stature of Christ. Thus growing, our influence on others, and on the environment in which we live, will be his influence, and odd as it may appear, we shall be assisting in that wonderful and sacred mystery, by means of which all things are returning to perfection, through him from whom they took their origin.

3

CHRIST

'CHRISTIANITY is Christ'—this is an old adage, the title of books, the subject of sermons. But it is such a vague and general statement that in itself it is virtually meaningless. Does it mean, for instance, that the essence of Christianity is the mere fact of Christ, the fact that he lived, and was who he was, and did what he did? Or does it mean that the essence of Christianity, for a Christian, is his or her attitude to Christ, and if so does this refer to his attitude to the Christ of history or to the Christ of faith—or both? —and are they the same thing? Usually, no doubt, the phrase is used to describe the attitude of mind which St. Paul referred to when he said 'To me to live is Christ' (Philippians 1. 21). But it is to give content and meaning to such an expression, and to give reasons for thinking like that, or trying to think like that, that this chapter is being written.

Let us begin by collecting a few basic facts about which there can be no dispute. They are indeed so familiar and obvious that it may seem unnecessary to write them down —yet it is not always easy to hold them together, in any kind of synthesis, or synoptic view.

The first is that the central, and longest, portions of the Apostles' and Nicene Creeds concern the person and work of our Lord Jesus Christ. The final parts of those Creeds concern the Holy Spirit and the Church and these matters are clearly derivative from faith in Christ. It can be said then that apart from the opening assertions concerning

God the Father (which could in general be shared with members of all theistic faiths) the whole of the Creeds concern Jesus. The distinguishing mark that is, of a Christian, as far as his belief is concerned, is what he believes about Christ, or better, whether or not he believes *in* him.

The second fact is this: of the literature which Christians have treasured and read as the 'New Testament', almost half consists of accounts of the life, death and resurrection of Jesus—in my Bible 116 pages out of 259. Another 35 pages tell the story of what happened immediately after his earthly life, and as this is set in contrast to the story of 'all that Jesus *began* both to do and teach' (Acts 1. 1) it is fair to assume that this is meant to be the story of what Jesus *continued* to do, through his apostles and his Church. The rest of the New Testament consists mostly of letters, formal and informal, which take us back to the life of the first Christians. Some of them were written before the Gospels took their present shape. All of them clearly assume that Jesus was afforded, in the circles where the letters were written and read, a status and importance quite different from that afforded to any other human being. He is constantly called Lord, Christ, Son of God and similar divine-sounding names. He is probably called 'Saviour' and possibly (in one or two slightly ambiguous places) is actually called God. He is, so to speak, 'bracketed' with God. He is pictured as seated on God's right hand in Heaven, destined 'to fill all things'.

A third fact, which is in a sense a development from what has been described in the last paragraph, is that with the development of the Doctrine of the Trinity, faith in Christ has been, as it were, conflated with faith in God. The earlier Creeds foreshadow this development in that they express belief in God the Father, in Jesus Christ his

Son, and in the Holy Spirit, but the formal expression of this threefold faith as faith in 'One God in Three Persons' came somewhat later than the period when these Creeds were taking shape. It had been hinted at, almost explicitly stated, in the New Testament (*see*, e.g. St. Matthew 28. 19 and 2 Corinthians 13. 14) but as a formal doctrine it is best looked for in documents like the so-called Athanasian Creed, perhaps a century later than the Nicene Creed. The reason for mentioning this matter at this early stage of a chapter on Christ is that many good Christians (particularly Anglican Christians) do not *isolate* belief in Christ from the rest of their faith. They believe in God, they believe in Christ as the Son of God and in the Holy Spirit, proceeding from the Father and the Son. Perhaps we should do better if in our worship and devotion we *did* pay more attention to faith *in Christ*. If we believe, as Christians do, that we see the glory of God in the face of Jesus Christ (2 Corinthians 4. 6) it is of supreme importance for us to 'turn our eyes upon Jesus'. 'Do you turn to Christ?' is the basic question in the new services of Baptism and Confirmation. One purpose of this chapter is to help readers to see what this question implies. We shall first have to consider a good deal more factual material, and look somewhat more closely at what has already been mentioned.

While postponing the question as to what authority need or can be ascribed to 'the tradition' which the Church cherishes about Jesus, there can be no harm, and possibly some good in having as clear a picture as possible of what that tradition is. To explain this I find myself thinking of those old parlour-toys common in my boyhood by means of which a double picture when looked at through this instrument (a 'stereoscope') merged into one vivid, apparently three-dimensional image. Similarly we have to look at Christ through two lenses, as it were, to get the whole picture.

One lens is that which is provided by the Gospels, especially those of St. Matthew, St. Mark, and St. Luke. Here we have three accounts, varying in detail and even in approach (as is apparent when they are closely studied by scholars) but to the ordinary eyes basically similar, in that they tell the story of Jesus—in two cases of his birth, and in all four cases of his baptism[1], of his teaching, of his miracles, of his passion and death, and of his resurrection. Granted that many Christians carry in their minds only a vague impression of all this, and others only selected incidents or sayings, it would be agreed by all who are capable of thinking about the matter that here is one immensely important 'strand' in the tradition. Closer study of course reveals that these 'gospels' are far from being neutral, objective statements about a first century Palestinian man: they are actually shot through with 'faith' as well as 'fact'. All the same, if we *should* be interested in looking at fact without faith, there is nowhere else to turn for basic material except to the Gospels. The factual information contained in the Epistles, though not to be despised when read alongside the Gospels, would be of very little value without them.

So much for the 'factual' lens. But from the earliest times, earlier in time than the final putting together of the Gospels, Christ had been looked at from a different point of view, or at least in a different perspective. Although it might be tempting to look at the early chapters of Acts for examples of this 'other' point of view, we will not do so because we are anxious to establish our case on the firmest possible foundations, foundations about which the

[1] St. John records the encounter between Jesus and the Baptist, but does not actually state that Jesus was baptised.

most radical Biblical critics cannot raise any objections. So we will go to the letters of St. Paul, to Galatians and Corinthians. We will omit even the letters to the Thessalonians, early as they probably are, because there are some critics who doubt their authenticity. The letter to the Galatians was written about A.D. 50, i.e. not more than twenty years after the events on which the Christian religion was founded, the death and resurrection of Jesus. Here is a letter the Pauline origin of which no one doubts. If Paul did not write Galatians, he never wrote anything. You can say, if you want to be clever, that Paul is the man who wrote Galatians, and that all other information about him (except that coming from the other undisputed letters) is secondary.

Open then Galatians at its first verses. Here we find that Paul regarded himself as 'an apostle', a 'sent one', of Jesus Christ and God the Father, who raised him from the dead. He sends grace and peace to the Churches of Galatia (proving that the movement was now well established in central Asia Minor). This grace and peace, he says, is 'from God the Father and from our Lord Jesus Christ'. So Jesus is not only Christ, (Messiah, anointed king) but 'Lord'. Here he is given the sacred name (*kurios*, the Greek equivalent of the Hebrew 'special' name for God, *Jahveh*). So at the least, Jesus has been 'bracketed' with God. The writer goes on 'who gave himself for our sins'—so his death is now treated as in some sense a sacrifice, in some way related to the sins of men. 'That he might deliver us from this present evil world, according to the will of God and our Father'—so the life, death, and resurrection of Jesus, looked at as a whole, is felt to be a means of deliverance, of salvation, from the situation in which men found themselves in the present world, which is described in brief as 'evil'. All this is 'according to the will of God'—it is no accident, it is no Prometheus-like act of defiance, it is all in accord with God's will and purpose.

Evidence of this sort can be culled from all the early Epistles. I Corinthians 12. 3 is important, for there we learn that the basic original Christian creed was 'Jesus is Lord'. So is I Corinthians 15. 1–8 where we have a more extended version of the primitive creed or gospel. This, we learn, began with the assertion that 'Christ' died for our sins and that this was in line with the teaching of the Old Testament ('according to the Scriptures'). 'He was buried, and rose again the third day'. (The close proximity of 'rose again' to 'buried' and the reference to the third day, suggests to me that Paul associated Christ's rising with leaving the tomb empty.) This should be remembered when those who disbelieve the stories concerning the empty tomb assert that 'Paul knew nothing of the empty tomb'[1]. After that he was seen of a whole list of witnesses, some being individuals, some large groups, the last being St. Paul himself ('he was seen of me also').

Now we just do not know how much of the information in the Gospels was known to St. Paul and his fellow-members of the primitive Church. We can point to limited statements in the Pauline and other letters that are *compatible* with their knowing a good deal. (The account of the Last Supper in I Corinthians 11. 23–26 lies very close to the accounts in the Synoptic Gospels.) But what *do* we know? We know that all the time the Epistles were being written the Gospels must have been taking shape. Both types of literature emerged in the Greek-speaking Christian church, although both epistles and gospels have Aramaic words embedded in them (e.g. 'Abba', Father, in St. Mark 14. 36 and in Romans 8. 15). It is clear that

[1] A note on the two 'special' miracles the Virgin Birth and the Empty Tomb, follows this chapter.

the 'Jesus' of whom St. Paul makes his striking assertions is the same Jesus of whom the Gospels tell. The two pictures can be looked at together. They reveal the same Christ.

A particular kind of fusion between the 'historic' and the 'dogmatic' is to be found in the Fourth Gospel. There is no opportunity here to go into this question in any detail. All I can say is that in general it gives 'a story of Jesus', a story clearly based on a tradition similar to that which lies behind the Synoptic Gospels, in spite of the many differences between 'St. John' and the other three Gospels. To put the agreement at the very lowest level, it is a story of a teacher, 'a Rabbi', who was at home in Galilee, who taught, healed, worked miracles, and who went up to Jerusalem, where he was crucified, and rose again. But the Jesus who lives this life is presented as knowing and claiming for himself, during his earthly life, the kind of divine status that is *assumed* to belong to him, rather than is asserted about him in the Epistles. The Fourth Gospel therefore contributes to the objectives of both the Gospels and the Epistles. It is a testimony to the primitive faith in Christ as the Revelation (or 'the Word') of God; it is also a clear testimony to the belief that the bearer of this revelation was a *man*, who lived and died in Palestine, as the other Gospels record.

By the end of the second century, when the Church was collecting the basic documents on which its faith was built, the Christian saw no difficulty in putting together, as it were in one volume, all the four Gospels, *and* most of the Epistles. The two pictures had fused to present one stereoscopic image.

The Creeds give us another sign of the way the faith of the Church in Christ was developing. The Apostles' Creed was taking shape by the end of the second century, the Nicene Creed by the early part of the fourth. A first glance at them will show that their *special* interest is in the broad perspective of the Epistles rather than in the details of the life of Jesus, such as we can read about in the Gospels. The section in the Apostles' Creed which concerns belief 'in Jesus Christ (God's) only Son our Lord' bears a close resemblance to the section already quoted from I Corinthians 15. Here then is a very brief summary of the main facts concerning Jesus considered in perspective. They are looked at from the point of view of their saving significance. So the statement begins by asserting the divine origin of Jesus Christ—He 'was conceived by the Holy Ghost, Born of the Virgin Mary'. These statements are either derived from the traditions embodied in the Birth narratives of St. Matthew and St. Luke, or from others similar to them. Then we go straight to the Passion—'He suffered under Pontius Pilate, was crucified, dead and buried'. Then to the Resurrection, Ascension, and the expected Return.

The Nicene Creed adds considerably to this very bald outline, but its additions do not concern the earthly life so much as the divine status of Jesus Christ. The form they finally took are the result of the Christological controversies of the fourth century, especially that in which Athanasius and Arius were the principal protagonists. So we find in the Nicene Creed of today the famous phrases 'God of God, Light of Light, Very God of Very God, begotten not made, being of *one substance* with the Father, (essence would have been a happier translation), by whom (this refers to Christ) all things were made.' All this is set in the context of our salvation—'Who *for us men and for our salvation* came down from heaven'. So by the time our Creeds took shape we have:

1 a fourfold record of the life-story of Jesus—not

biographies in the modern sense, rather four different versions of the same 'good news', hence called 'Gospels';

2 first century letters which show how the whole of this story, looked at as a unity, with special concentration on the Cross and Resurrection, was seen, at latest within twenty years of its ending, and in fact long before that interval had elapsed, as a mighty act of God. This act was so unique and so full of God-given significance, that the principal character in it, Jesus of Nazareth, had to be 'included' in the Godhead, first as 'Lord', but also as Son of God, Word of God, and Saviour;

3 summaries of Christian faith, preserved to our day and still in use, commonly called the Apostles' Creed and the Nicene Creed, where, in the language of those ancient times, the *meaning* of the life, death, and resurrection of Jesus was set out, not in cold theological statements, but in terms of commitment, of confession of personal faith— 'We believe *in* his only Son our Lord—we believe these things about him, but most of all we commit and trust ourselves to him of whom we believe these things.'

Allowing for necessary abbreviations and simplifications I believe the preceding pages to set out facts of Christian history which all reasonable men would agree to—not of course that they would necessarily agree with *what* was said or thought, but that at least these things *were* said and thought at those times and in those places. I believe it is necessary from time to time to set out these facts clearly so that we all, believers, half-believers, and non-believers can in a book such as this all start from the same base line.

We now turn to a much more significant and immediate question—What are *we* to think about Christ? Can *we* say, 'I believe in Jesus Christ, his only Son, our Lord'? And if

35

we can, why can we do so, and what do we mean when we say it?

Where do *we* start when we think about our relation to Christ? Let us begin by facing a few problems which, if left on one side, can create confusion and misunderstanding. It is not given to everybody, as I have already hinted, to *isolate* their religious attitude to Christ from all the rest of their religious experience. Anglicans, for instance, have been bred in a Church where the Psalms are very much used. Some of them may be interpreted in a Christian sense (e.g. the 23rd psalm, 'The Lord is my shepherd', may be blended in the mind with the Gospel picture of Christ as the Good Shepherd). But a piety nourished on the Psalms will remain in all probability a God-centred, rather than a Christ-centred piety. Again, many people do not take too easily to the 'stereoscopic' blend of the historic Jesus and the Christ of faith. They may set themselves to 'follow Christ', to cultivate the *imitatio Christi*, but they may not so easily visualise the living Christ, ascended yet present, as the object of their present-day prayer and worship. Yet again, not all Christians easily distinguish between Christ as a separate 'Person', (if you like, the Second Member of the Holy Trinity) and Christ as he makes himself known in concrete, contemporary situations, in the fellowship of the Church, or in cases of contemporary human need. We have his own authority for believing that he is 'present' under both such sets of circumstances—'Where two or three are gathered together in my name there am I in the midst'; and 'In as much as ye did it (or did it not) unto one of the least of these my brethren, ye did it (or did it not) unto me.'

So we must admit that there is a wide variety of 'modes' in which the individual can visualise (or 'externalise') his relation to Christ. It is possible that any one of those mentioned may be a legitimate starting-point, and I think that lengthening experience and growing maturity in discipleship tend towards a more comprehensive, many-sided conception of faith in Christ, rather than the reverse. In any case we should think of the relationship between 'the Church' and Christ as more significant than that between the Christian and Christ. There will always be endless varieties of personal and individual experience. The experience of the Church on the other hand, is classical and decisive: it is for the Christian to grow into *that*, and to share it as fully as he can.

So it is, then, that *in practice*, there is no limit to the different situations and circumstances that may provide the starting-point of Christian experience and Christian faith. There are the standard 'initiations' of the Church, Holy Baptism, early Christian education, family tradition, Confirmation. Even when these do not immediately yield the fruit of personal faith they may provide the back-ground against which, years later, something positive may emerge. Other events which may take a potential Chris-tian some way along the road to articulate personal faith are the preliminaries to marriage, the birth of the first child, the Confirmation of children, enlistment in church enterprises such as Stewardship Campaigns, efforts for those in need, such as are undertaken by Christian Aid, Oxfam, or Shelter. The principal factor in all such cases is not the event itself, but the fact that the event brings the 'enquirer' (if such he be) into personal touch with committed Christians (often, but not always, the ordained minister). This contact causes a breakdown of those barriers which so easily cut off our people from public worship and Christian commitment. So it is that once inside the Christian community the seeker begins to hear what is said there, to do what is done there, and at last to love and serve the Lord who there is loved and served. Even so, there will be great differences between the way in which individuals will articulate their faith, particularly as this relates to 'belief in the Lord Jesus Christ'.

If, from this point of view, I had to articulate my own faith in a limited number of words, I should say something like this: 'I trust in, and seek to obey, God, who is made real to me in Jesus Christ, incarnate, crucified, and risen, present in the Church, active in the world, always calling me to closer discipleship as he called and re-called his disciples while on earth.' Because he represents so fully 'the mind of God' I can say 'all things were made by him', and because God's purpose is wrapped up in him, I can say 'his kingdom shall have no end'.

In ways such as this one can pass from the kind of 'localised' interest in individual events recorded in the Gospels, and the all-inclusive statements about Christ asserted in the Creeds, statements which do not fall short of naming him as 'God of God'.

We may say then that the Christian Church (and all Christians in so far as they grow into the classical faith of the Church) sees Christ in God and God in Christ, and that the human delineaments of Christ are provided by the records of his deeds and words as these are found in the Gospels. I think it is well worthwhile, even at the cost of some repetition, to clarify as far as possible the relation between, even the tension between, the Christ of the Gospels and the Christ of the Creeds. This is necessary, I believe, as a first step, before people can be helped to come to terms with the difficult formulations concerning 'the two natures' of Christ. Article 2 of the 39 Articles, following the Athanasian Creed and the so-called Chalcedonian Definition, says that in Christ 'two whole and perfect Natures, that is to say the Godhead and the Manhood,

were joined together in one Person, never to be divided
. . . .' The difficulty with this language, which is lifted
almost entire from the fifth century, is that it assumes that
we know quite clearly what 'Godhead' is, and what 'Manhood' is. It is not unreasonable to think that we have *some*
idea of what manhood is (although it is a Christian insight that *only* in Christ do we see 'the proper Man', and
a philosophical insight that manhood can only be per-
ceived in the moment-by-moment experience of being
man) but it is more hazardous to think that we can define
'Godhead' with any degree of accuracy. The difficulty,
however, for most thoughtful Christians does *not* rest in
any doubt that the Creeds and Councils were right in
insisting that Christ bridged *both* sides of the God–Man
divide. His manhood has not usually been in doubt (although in trying to understand his Deity the manhood
has sometimes been almost extinguished) but there have
been times (and this is one of them) when doubts have
been expressed as to whether he was 'Very God'. Classical
Christian thought has held, and still holds, that Christ's
saving work could not be guaranteed unless *his* action
was God's action, unless *God* was in Christ reconciling the
world to himself, unless we can believe that nothing shall
separate us from the love of God which is in Christ Jesus
our Lord.

Although I have been at pains to lay stress on the
unique, all-inclusive redeeming act of God in Christ, I
also believe that individual Christians will lay hold of, or
be laid hold of by, Christ, as he is brought before us in the
Gospels. I intend now to mention six different 'moments'
or groupings of Gospel material which help different
people to begin a life of definite discipleship.

There are the Christmas stories. These have the curious
feature of being known and loved by the largest

39

proportion of all those owning any Christian allegiance while raising more questions than most of the other Gospel material in the minds of careful historically-minded critics. It is clearly impossible in a short book, with the perspective here taken up, to deal in detail with the points of apparent difference between the stories in St. Matthew and St. Luke, or with the major question of 'the supernatural' which plays (like lightning over the countryside) over 'the natural' in all the Birth narratives. But this can be said. These are stories which at quite an early date in Christian history (e.g. around A.D. 85) were loved and treasured as vivid embodiments of the truth of the Incarnation. This was how Christians of those days saw the first beginnings of God's mighty intervention in history—in the birth of a helpless baby in an outcast family. Some in every age have been moved by the same stories, and experience suggests that they can do their work quite apart from complicated arguments about the historical status of this detail or that.

There are some who will always give first place in their thinking about Christ to his teaching. This is preserved for us in striking form in the so-called Sermon on the Mount (St. Matthew 5, 6, and 7) and in the many parables scattered through the Gospels. St. John gives many chapters of teaching, in which the 'I am' sayings are prominent, and which reach a climax in the 'farewell speeches' of chapters 14, 15, 16, and 17. The outstanding feature of Christ's teaching is not, rather surprisingly, its originality, for much of it can be paralleled either in the Old Testament or in rabbinical sources. Its striking features are its direct authority, its immediacy, and its penetration. Jesus taught that the rule or realm of God (commonly called 'the kingdom of God' or 'the kingdom of Heaven') was 'at hand', just round the corner, already available to any who would submit gladly and trustfully to its sway. It was a rule where God's goodness and love prevailed. Those who entered into it must be ready to love and forgive as they had been forgiven. This teaching was expressed in a large number of never-to-be-forgotten stories, riddles, conundrums, or whatever name you prefer for the 'parables'. The 'down-to-earthness' of the parables, their continual use of the commonest situations in home, family and farm is not just a coincidence. Surely it implies that the whole world is God's world, and that life's secret is to look on every happening as having within it a kernel, which if only we could discern it, points the way to God's rule, in which is our happiness and our peace. The 'teaching' is vital. St. Matthew saw it as waiting to be imparted to all the nations (St. Matthew 28. 20).

Then we come to the miracles, which present a different kind of problem. No one need doubt that Christ gave the teaching that is ascribed to him: the difficulty is to carry it out. No one is expected to carry out similar miracles to Christ's: the problem is, did they happen?

Let me give an example of the problem as it arises in the minds of modern men (and Christians are also modern men!). When I first took a party to the Holy Land I stopped the bus as we came in sight of the blue waters of the Sea of Galilee. It was a never-to-be-forgotten moment for all of us Christian pilgrims. But one elderly lady, with tears streaming down her face, said, 'And to think that Our Lord walked on that water!' Strange as it may seem, that remark threw me up sharply against the question, 'Did he really?' It is easy to live all one's life with a vague acceptance of the wonderful miracle stories without asking oneself too plainly 'if we had been there, should we have seen things like that?'

Modern books on the miracles, such as Alan Richardson's *Miracle-Stories of the Gospels* (S.C.M., 1941), place much stress on the theological *meaning* of the miracles, reminding us of the many Old Testament texts that seem to prepare the way for them. (e.g. 'He shall feed his flock like a shepherd'—preparing for the miraculous feedings; 'Then shall the eyes of the blind be opened'—preparing for the curing of the blind men.) But these interpretations, while enlightening and enriching, make more difficult rather than less so, the historical questions that nag at the mind of our contemporaries. Do they not supply a possible motive which may have led to the 'invention' or modification of the material?

I can make only one or two brief points in this context. First of all I would mention that 'miracles' (marvel-making events) are embedded in the very texture of the earliest records. You cannot *remove* from Mark, or any of the Gospels, the stories of the healing of lepers, demoniacs, lame and blind, without leaving yourself with a story that does not hang together. This in itself does not solve the problem, but it bars the way to one possible escape route. Secondly, there are a sufficient number of *apparently* irreconcilable details as between the Gospels to make a one-hundred-per-cent acceptance of every single detail virtually impossible for an honest enquirer. Thirdly, it is possible to believe that what seemed a totally inexplicable miracle then, in the light of a more scientific approach to the same phenomena, might be capable of a less 'miraculous' explanation. If for instance a first century man had been confronted with radio, television, or radar, how would he have described or explained it? My own view, therefore, and I claim no special authority for it, is that many wonderful things happened as a result of the words and works of Jesus. Some of them may have happened much as we read of them: in others pious imagination, and what we should now call 'pulpit-use' may have contributed much. But if what we assert in quite other contexts, is true, (viz. that 'God was in Christ') and that this 'was-ness' was unique in character, so unique as to justify us in calling Jesus 'his only Son our Lord', it would be really more surprising if his ordinary life had *not* been marked by many events quite unlike those that normally surround *our* ordinary lives. In spite of all this, the miracles, which in times past were one of the most powerful arguments for 'the divinity of Christ', are for many more of a difficulty to be surmounted than a solution to be welcomed.

An aspect of the Gospel-story not always emphasised, but precious to me, is the picture that emerges of Christ's dealing with individuals. When all allowance has been made for literary adjustments, and pious 'throw-backs' from the post-Resurrection period, it is remarkable how one can trace real personal encounters between Jesus and Peter, Jesus and the woman with the haemorrhage, Jesus and the children, Jesus and the woman taken in adultery, and many other cases. In the light of modern thought about the importance of personal relationships, this is an aspect of 'the face of Jesus Christ' to which it will be legitimate to pay more attention in the future than in the past.

What can one say in a few lines about the Passion and the Cross? One can say at least this: here was the centre of the story in the mind of the first Christians. Strange would a modern biography be if more than a third of the space was devoted to the last week of the life (as is the case with St. Mark). Only in connection with the Passion and the Cross is there any kind of hour-by-hour chronicle. It is reasonable to believe that the final chapters of the Gospels present us with the kind of material that was told again and again at the regular celebrations of the Eucharist. (cf. I Corinthians 11. 26. 'As often as ye eat this bread, and drink this cup, ye "tell forth" the Lord's death, till he come.') Even as a story of purely human courage, patience, and sacrifice, it would stand out perhaps uniquely, in the long story of human suffering and martyrdom. But such arguments are precarious. Tastes and standards vary, and even if the past could yield no parallel, the future might. No, the uniqueness of the Cross depends not on the human achievement, but on the divine meaning which it almost immediately came to bear. It was in the Cross that followers of Jesus almost immediately came to see the proof and indication of God's redeeming love. 'God commendeth his love to us in that while we were yet sinners, Christ died for us' (Romans 5. 8). It is in the 'for us' (cf. Luther's stress on the *pro me*) that the *special* appeal of the Cross lies.

The Gospels end with the story of the Resurrection. Again it is difficult, indeed impossible, to smooth away all the minor discrepancies between the stories. I do not say that no ingenuity *could* succeed in doing so, but it can be done only by allowing a degree of special pleading that we should not allow to our opponents. All the same, taken together, the Gospels give us a wonderful picture of what 'the third day' was like—a day that opened in gloom and sadness, and ended in dazed joy and wonder. Something very like what is here described is needed to explain the uninhibited confidence with which the earliest Christian letters refer to the fact that 'God raised him from the dead'.

Stirred to interest, and then to commitment, by one or all of these 'episodes', or by others here not noted, the Christian comes to bow his knee to the name of Jesus, and to give him the Name which is above every name. The process may be gradual, or it may be sudden and decisive.

Its content may be clearly articulated, or it may be vague and largely a 'song without words'. It is an attitude to life, growing out of a commitment of the mind and heart and will. It needs continual support from reading, from worship, from sacrament, from active engagement in Christ's service day by day.

A note on the two 'Special' Miracles

It is necessary to pay special attention to the two 'special' miracles recorded in the Gospels—the Virgin Birth and the Empty Tomb. It is noteworthy that these concern the beginning and the end of the earthly story of Jesus, the first concerning his arrival in human history, the second his disappearance from normal human sight. They constitute 'stumbling-blocks' for many sympathetic but scientifically-minded Christians of today. The writer of this book has been told quite plainly that 'no one can be expected to believe those things nowadays', and this has been used as an introduction to a statement of deep interest in, and attachment to, the teaching of Our Lord.

Each of these miracles must be treated separately. The only link between them is the fact that both events are out of line with all other known human experience, and that they both concern the marginal territory between the earthly life of our Lord Jesus Christ, and whatever preceded and followed it.

THE VIRGIN BIRTH

It is commonly pointed out that this event is recorded only in the Gospels of Matthew and Luke. Neither Mark nor John mention it, although there may be a hint of it in St. John 8. 41 where 'the Jews' say to Jesus 'We were not born of fornication', a possible suggestion that something unusual was believed to have accompanied his

45

birth. It is necessary to point out further that the only two Gospels which record the birth at all record a *Virgin* Birth. There is no reference to the Virgin Birth in the Epistles, but again there is virtually no reference to the birth at all except in Galatians 4. 4, 'God sent forth his Son, born of a woman, born under the law'. It has to be said that there are considerable divergencies between the story in Matthew and that in Luke, but both agree that the mother of Jesus was Mary, and that Mary's betrothed, Joseph, was not the father of Jesus, though he was at Mary's side through the infancy and early childhood of the Lord. By the time the Canon began to take shape, both Matthew and Luke were admitted to it, and no one took exception to the infancy narratives of these two Gospels. On the contrary, the Virgin Birth at once took its place as an integral part of the basic Creeds. The earliest Roman creeds we know have as one of their clauses 'And in Christ Jesus his only son, our Lord, who was born of the Holy Spirit and the Virgin Mary'. It could be said that no particular stress was laid on the virginity of Mary, and that the word 'Virgin' when attached to her was little more than a title. But at the very least this shows that during the time between the acceptance of Matthew and Luke and the formation of these early Creeds, thought about Mary had been based on the stories in Matthew and Luke. The Virgin Birth had become part of the tradition.

So we must go *behind* the Gospels if we want further light. Here we can say that as the stories in Matthew and Luke vary in important particulars, they must both go back to a point where what is common to them both was 'received tradition'. As both books emerged at about A.D. 85–95 it would seem that the common 'core'—the fact of the Virgin Birth itself—must have been accepted by about 65 at the latest. At that date many must have still been alive who knew Our Lord, and possibly even his mother. If there is substance in the tradition that Mary went to Ephesus, her news and information would have been fed right into the main stream of first century Christianity. The balance of this evidence suggests to me that the tradition as we have it may well be authentic, but as purely historical evidence what we have is not widespread enough, or incontestably authentic enough, to suppress all doubts and questions.

We then are faced with the question whether it is legitimate for a modern Christian to be disbelieving or agnostic about a point in the Creed which has been there ever since there were such things as Creeds. If it became evident that the material in the Gospels (and hence in the Creeds) was manifestly legendary or bogus, we should have to consider the resulting position. I could say myself that if the strong and vigorous faith of the early Christians gave rise to poetic fancies, based possibly on misunderstanding of Old Testament phrases ('A virgin shall conceive' in Isaiah 7. 14 is already reduced to 'a young woman is with child' in the New English Bible), it would still be possible to use the credal language to express the *same* faith in Christ as God's unique Son as it was meant to express in the first centuries. The historic fact would not be absolutely vital. A difficulty would arise from the fact that no part of our traditional faith laid hold more completely on the medieval mind than the story of the babe of Bethlehem and his virgin mother. To persuade half Christendom to sing its Christmas Carols in a different sense would be no mean task. For myself I feel able still to say 'Born of the Virgin Mary' and mean it. I do not feel the Virgin Birth to be necessary to a belief in the sinlessness of Christ, or in his divine and unique sonship. The part played by Our Lord's mother seems to me to raise all the questions that would be raised by a normal paternity. But I find the belief embedded in the faith as soon as that faith emerges from the 'tunnel' between the Resurrection and the emergence of the early documents of the faith. I find every reason to accept the rest, and am ready to accept this, as part of a 'package deal'. Once one does accept it, one sees many points which make it consonant with all the rest that we believe. We believe that God was engaged in a decisive step in the redemption of the world, and nothing symbolises this better than the story which tells of a new beginning in man's history. Perhaps it symbolises it so well because this is how God did in fact achieve his purpose.

THE EMPTY TOMB

It may surprise some readers to be told that the evidence for the Empty Tomb—the sheer, hard, historical evidence —is a good deal stronger than that for the Virgin Birth. For one thing it is found in all four Gospels, instead of in only two of them. As there are divergences, the common element must date from a time well before the date of the earliest of them, viz. St. Mark (A.D. 65). Furthermore, it being obvious that Jesus was born *somehow* (i.e. either with a normal paternity, or not) the point at issue is whether he was born in *one* way, rather than another. With the Resurrection, assuming that *something* happened, *that something* was clearly a miracle, something unlike any other event in human history. Now it is possible to believe in 'the Resurrection' and not to believe in the Empty Tomb. But as all who believe in the Resurrection at all have to believe in a staggering miracle, it is not much more difficult to believe in one which involves the matter of the dead body, than in one which does not. The whole of the New Testament (and of course the Creeds) assume or assert that 'God raised Jesus from the dead'. The burden of proof *for believers* lies with those who believe that he did so, but that he did so in a way totally different from that which is embedded in the earliest documents. I personally feel that the Hebrew sense of unity between the body and the spirit was so strong that I doubt whether the first Christians could have believed in the Resurrection without the evidence of the Empty Tomb. *We* might have done, but not they.

4

THE SPIRIT AND THE CHURCH

AT FIRST sight it may seem strange that one chapter should be made to cover two such enormous subjects—and particularly strange that 'the Spirit'—the Holy Spirit, the Third Person of the Holy Trinity—should be bracketed with 'the Church', which is to many an all-too-human institution. But there is good reason for taking the two subjects in very close proximity to each other. 'The Spirit in the New Testament is indissolubly connected with the Church'—so wrote W. R. Matthews in *God in Christian Thought and Experience* (Nisbet, 1930, p. 185) and indeed this is so. On the very last page of the New Testament we read (Revelation 22. 17), 'The Spirit and the Bride say, Come', and here 'the Bride' means the Church. It is a cry of hope and expectation addressed to the Lord: the cry of the Church, inspired by the Spirit, calling for the return of the Bridegroom, her Lord and Saviour. Such thoughts are not confined to ancient writers. The Reverend George Bennett, the President of the Divine Healing Mission, wrote as follows in a circular newsletter (April, 1970): 'The strange impression made on me is that a new Church is emerging. We are all aware to the changes taking place in patterns of worship, in new Bible transla-tions, in new designs for Church buildings with their emphasis on congregational participation in worship, in ecumenical witness and discussion. These are outward signs of a deep change within. This is a new age of the Holy Spirit where, I believe, the "Bride" is being prepared for the coming of the "Bridegroom".' It is not necessary either to assent to, or to differ from, Mr. Bennett's evaluation of contemporary changes in Church life to see the significance of his recognition of the close link still existing between 'the Spirit and the Bride'.

Furthermore, it is in some mysterious way characteristic of the activity of the Holy Spirit to be self-effacing. It would of course be wickedly irreverent to think that we could in any way postulate any grace or virtue of any one Member of the Holy Trinity that did not equally belong to the other Persons, for all are in every way equal. It yet is true that in their function, in their relationship to us men and our salvation different graces are brought into prominence, and the *particular* grace which Scripture associates with the Holy Spirit is the fact that he points men to Christ, the Son. 'He shall take of mine, and shall show it unto you', says Our Lord of the Spirit in St. John 16. 14. 'No man can say "Jesus is Lord" but in the Holy Spirit' says St. Paul in I Corinthians 12. 3. St. Augustine had the rather mysterious idea that the Being of the Spirit in some way finds expression in the *love* that binds together the Father and the Son. We are not ready yet to make any sweeping 'metaphysical' assertions on these difficult subjects, but mention them only to show that a chapter where 'The Spirit' is treated in close proximity to the Church which is his creation and the sphere of his influence is not theologically inappropriate.

We say in the Creed, 'I believe in the Holy Ghost'— why do we so believe, and what does it mean so to believe? The English (and the Anglican) mind works historically, so we can begin by looking at the early days of the Church, and by trying to discover how it was that Christians ever said things like that. The most sceptical radical has to admit that people called Christians did express belief in 'the Holy Ghost', and there must have been a reason for this, good or bad.

Once more we must begin with an 'undisputed' saying, and we cannot do better than start with one of the most familiar verses in the Bible, II Corinthians 13. 14: 'The grace of the Lord Jesus Christ, and the love of God and the fellowship (or communion) of the Holy Spirit be with you all'. Thus says St. Paul, writing about A.D. 55. One can understand at once why he should refer to 'the grace of our Lord Jesus Christ'; the whole Christian movement depended on the gracious act of Christ in living and dying for men. 'Ye know the grace of our Lord Jesus Christ, how that though He was rich yet for our sakes he became poor.' The apostle wanted his readers to enter more and more fully into what this meant. One can understand why he referred to 'the love of God'. It was God's love which the Cross had brought to men: 'God commendeth his love to us in this, that while we were yet sinners Christ died for us'. But why go on to 'the fellowship of the Holy Spirit'? Surely because this fellowship, this sharing was already felt to be a vital element in the whole Christian experience, an element which no less than the grace and the love brought Christians into touch with the living God, this time known and experienced as 'the Holy Spirit'. We know from other writings of St. Paul how essential in all Christian experience was the presence and power of the Spirit. We have already seen that it was only through the power and assistance of the Spirit that any one could confess that 'Jesus is Lord'. The eighth chapter of Romans throws light on many aspects of the Spirit's influence as St. Paul understood it. According to him the Spirit of God 'dwelt in' the Christians (verse 8). Those who were led by the Spirit of God were the sons of God (verse 14).

The Spirit enables Christians to use the same word of

affectionate trust in their prayers to God as Jesus himself had used, the word 'Abba' (verse 15). This led St. Paul to describe the Spirit as 'the spirit of adoption', or of sonship. The Spirit confirmed the conviction of the Christians that they really were the sons of God (verse 16). The Spirit 'took over' the prayers of Christians (which otherwise would be made in floundering ignorance) 'because he maketh intercession for the saints according to the will of God' (verse 27). All these statements, and many others like them, show that to the first Christians, their experience of God in Christ was made real, personal and contemporary by an influence to which they gave the name of 'the Spirit'. Sometimes he was called 'the Spirit of God' sometimes 'the Spirit of Christ', sometimes 'the Holy Spirit', sometimes just 'the Spirit'. God's revelation had come 'through the Spirit' (I Corinthians 2. 10). The Spirit searched 'the deep things of God' (same verse). None but the Spirit knew these deep things. The 'things of the Spirit of God' were not open to 'the natural man', but only to 'the spiritual' i.e. to those in whom the Spirit of God was the regnant force.

Now what is important to remember is that all this was based on experience. It may have been wrongly interpreted experience, but it was experience. By A.D. 55 this was how Greek-speaking Christians felt and spoke about the Spirit.

The Fourth Gospel provides another mine of information about the way some Christians at least thought about the Holy Spirit. While scholars may argue and discuss the exact date and provenance of St. John's Gospel we shall be on fairly safe ground if we treat it as coming from the end of the first century, and representing a distinct but not wildly unorthodox picture of Christian faith. Its language and style were distinctive, but not so distinctive as to make it impossible for it to be put alongside the other Gospels, 'bound up with them', as we should say today.

53

Three other writings in the same style, (the three 'Epistles of John') were also included in the Canon of New Testament writings by the time of Athanasius. Now whether we believe that in St. John we have the *ipsissima verba* of Jesus, or whether we think of it as representing a mature 'meditation' on the life-giving power of Jesus, in which he is made to speak from his lips what was really the Church's confession of faith in him as the Way, the Truth and the Life, the Gospel still represents what *some* Christians felt and believed at the time the Gospel was written. In this light we can see what those Christians believed about the Holy Spirit. In the so-called Farewell Speeches (chapters 14–17 inclusive) we find the clearest teaching in the New Testament about the Holy Spirit. Here we learn that it is the function of the Spirit to carry on the work of Jesus—as we have been reminded, Jesus says of him, 'He shall take of mine, and shall show it unto you'. He will lead the disciples into all truth (16. 13). He will teach them all things, and 'bring to their remembrance all that he had said unto them' (14. 25). He will 'abide in them', 'be with them for ever' (14. 16). He will carry 'convicting' power (16. 8). He is continually described by the Greek word *ekeinos*, which is a *personal* pronoun.

It is only after studying the significance of theological statements of this kind that it is helpful to go back to the 'narrative' statements of the Acts, and to those of the Synoptic Gospels. If we want to take a severely cautious view of the evidence, we can believe that the stories of the Spirit's coming at Pentecost, in Acts 2, and some of the sayings about the Spirit attributed to Jesus in the Synoptic Gospels (e.g. St. Luke 11. 13: 'how much more shall your Heavenly Father give the Holy Spirit to them that ask him?) are carrying back into the past insights and convictions which had only become real to them during the post-Easter years. (Professor C. K. Barrett's book, *The Holy Spirit and the Gospel Tradition* takes this view.) But if we hold this view, we are positing still more evidence as to the reality and certainty of *that* experience. And it is possible that the form the stories took reflected the kind of experience the Christians had—that they had discovered that the Spirit within them enabled them to preach Christ crucified and risen with convincing effect; that he brought unity, joy, and love into their corporate experience; that he was a safe and sure Guide to them in their Christian activities (*see* Acts 16. 6); that he could be 'a mighty rushing wind' or 'a still small voice'. It is clear that his relation to Christ was thought of as very close. He was called 'the spirit of Jesus'. St. Paul once said 'the Lord *is* the Spirit', and scholars have been debating ever since exactly what he meant by that cryptic phrase.

Well, that is a fair enough account, I believe, of the thought of the primitive Church about the Spirit. How about us? Can we, dare we, must we also say, 'I believe in the Holy Spirit'? We can, and we must, but God, who sees all, will understand if we need help and patience before we can share with full confidence the thought and language of the early days on this aspect of our faith.

'No man hath seen God at any time'—true enough, but perhaps we can say without irreverence that the Holy Spirit is the most 'invisible' Person of the Holy Trinity. God the Father has his visible 'sign' in the heavens themselves. 'The heavens declare the glory of God: and the firmament sheweth his handiwork.' We saw in chapter 1 the problems involved in arguing from nature to God, but we also saw the abiding force of the old classical arguments. I for one can still sing with conviction Joseph Addison's great verses expanding Psalm 19. Writing of 'the radiant orbs' moving round 'in solemn silence' he goes on:

55

In reason's ear they all rejoice,
And utter forth a glorious voice;
For ever singing as they shine,
'The hand that made us is Divine'

In this sense, at least, God has not left himself without witness.

Our Lord has come forth out of the eternal darkness and has made his tent or tabernacle in history: the Word was made flesh. So there is no difficulty (I speak in broad, general terms) about visualising him. We can see real features in 'the face of Jesus Christ', and for these features we depend primarily upon the Gospels. The difficulty, if such there be, consists in how to think clearly about the relation between 'the Jesus of History' and the Eternal Son, or Word of God.

When it comes to the Holy Spirit, where do human eyes and ears look for signs of his activity? In the Old Testament men called it 'Spirit of God' when strange and wonderful things happened. Primeval chaos reduced to order, prophets half-frenzied with spiritual excitement, mighty deeds of valour—all these could be put down to the coming of the Spirit of God upon nature or upon men. But some at least of the Old Testament teachers saw the influence of the Spirit in more personal, more ethical terms. The most famous example is the passage in which Isaiah pictured the coming Judge, 'the shoot out of the stock of Jesse' as being endowed with manifold gifts from 'the spirit of the Lord'—a spirit of wisdom and understanding, a spirit of counsel and might, a spirit of knowledge and of the fear of the Lord (Isaiah 11). By a very slight expansion (the addition of 'true godliness' to knowledge) the list of gifts was built up to seven, and the language was taken over for use in the main Confirmation prayer of the Church, and for the Whitsun hymns ('Come, thy seven-fold gifts impart').

There is no doubt that the primitive Church felt itself to be the recipient of a great endowment of 'Holy Spirit'. Often his presence was associated with evangelistic advance, and with 'the gift of tongues' which plays so big a part in the story of the Day of Pentecost in Acts 2. More important, however, in the long run was the insight that the production of Christian *character* was 'the fruit of the Spirit'. So we come to St. Paul's 'nine-fold' picture of the Spirit's fruit in Galatians 5. 22–23: 'The fruit of the Spirit is love, joy, peace, long suffering, gentleness, goodness, fidelity, meekness, self-control'. The bass of the Old Testament needs to be balanced by the sweet treble of the New, if we are to learn the full music of the Spirit-filled life.

This conception of the Spirit as 'God-at-work-in-the-Church-and-in-individual-lives' has never been wholly lost, but the Church has only itself to blame for not treasuring it more carefully and exploring its depth more fully. The *formal*, institutional side of it has been the best preserved. For most of the centuries of Christian history, Baptism has been completed, either at the time or later, by some kind of Confirmation, to sacramentalise the promise of the Spirit as available for every Christian. Ordination has contained the words: 'Receive ye the Holy Ghost for the office and work of a Priest (or Bishop) in the Church of God' thus making permanent the New Testament insight that all the gifts by which the life of the Church is maintained are gifts of the Holy Spirit (I Corinthians 12). The festival of Whitsuntide, less markedly observed than Christmas or Easter, has *just* reminded the Church year by year that there *is* a Holy Spirit. But the price for a *comparative* neglect of him and his gifts is seen in

57

the vast proliferation of Pentecostal sects throughout the world.

As early as the third century the main (Catholic) Church had to cope with this problem, and no less a person than Tertullian became a 'Montanist', the name then given to a kind of extreme Pentecostalism. If, however, we would be true to the Catholic tradition at its best we shall say, in the words of the Athanasian Creed, 'The Father is God, the Son is God: and the Holy Ghost is God. And yet they are not three Gods: but one God.'

Perhaps we feel more cautious than our fathers did about being too cut-and-dried, too dogmatic, about things that by their nature lie far beyond the horizon of the human mind. The best Christians have always felt a proper reserve about things like this. 'Dangerous it were' wrote Richard Hooker, 'for the feeble brain of man to wade far into the doings of the Most High; whom although to know be life, and joy to make mention of his name; yet our soundest knowledge is to know that we know Him not as indeed he is, neither can know him: and our safest eloquence concerning him is our silence, when we confess without confession that his glory is inexplicable, his greatness above our capacity and reach. He is above, and we upon earth; therefore it behoveth our words to be wary and few' (*Laws of Ecclesiastical Polity:* Bk. I, Chs. 2, 3. Keble Edition, Vol. 1, p. 201).

It is not an easy task to build up—as from outside the experience of Christians and the Church—an intellectually convincing case for the Deity of the Holy Spirit. It is not really surprising that this was the last great doctrinal battle to be fought out in the early centuries, and that documents like the *Gloria in Excelsis* and the *Te Deum* were too early to give the Holy Spirit space and place equal to that given to the Father and the Son. What *can* be said is that those Christians who have lived most closely to God, the saints in every age, have been those to whom the personality and divinity of the Spirit have been most real. The experience lying behind the Whitsun hymns is real experience. We *may* think we can interpret their experience in more restrained or cautious language than their authors used. I for my part am prepared to believe that their experience of God in Christ is greater than mine, and while I try to follow them in their experience, I am ready to use their language, the language of the Church in the matter of this doctrine. It is a case of saying with St. Anselm, *Credo ut intelligam*—I believe, in order that I may understand.

And now what of 'the Church'? For in the Creed we say that we believe in One, Holy, Catholic, Apostolic Church. In the Creed, faith in the Church follows quickly upon faith in the Holy Spirit, for the Church is the sphere in which the Holy Spirit's power and influence are known. 'The world cannot receive (him) for the world neither sees nor knows him. But you know him, because he dwells with you, and shall be in you' (St. John 14. 17). But few 'items' in the Creed are under such heavy fire as this. The difficulty of 'believing in the Church' has of course long been recognised. 'I believe in the Holy Catholic Church', said William Temple, 'and I regret that it does not exist.' That was his epigrammatic way of pointing out the wide gap between the ideal Church—(one, holy, catholic, and apostolic) and the actual Church—divided, sinful, localised, and inward-looking, as it is all too often found to be. But things have moved a great deal even since Temple's day. The catholicity and apostolicity of the Church have in fact been much more seriously sought after than in earlier decades. Great strides have been made toward greater charity if not towards greater unity. The sense of *mission* is much more widely felt—witness Christian Aid and Oxfam. On the other hand 'the Church' has come in for some really devastating criticism. An American has called the Church 'the grave of God'. You could not have anything more damning than that. To anyone who has seen in the Church 'the pillar and ground of the truth', the base from which the Gospel spreads far and wide, Jerusalem on earth, 'Zion, city of our God' such a description cannot but be felt to be almost blasphemous. But it is useless to be shocked. We must look again at the part the Church has played in the outworking of God's purpose, and the part it still has to play.

If we *do* 'believe in the Church' what does it mean? What *is* there to believe in, whether or not we are right to believe in it?

There is first of all, an architectural heritage. This is an aspect of the Church's life that makes less appeal today than ever before. The great financial burden of maintaining the churches as buildings seems to many, especially those of the younger generation, to impede the Church's *mission*, whether considered as the mission of evangelism or the mission of service to a hungry and needy third world. It is still possible however to look back over the sixteen centuries during which church-building has been allowed, and to wonder at the varied expression in stone and brick which Christian faith has inspired and Christian worship necessitated. To have travelled, as many now have done, from Bethlehem, where the Church of the Nativity takes one back to the first buildings of Christian history under Constantine and Helena; to Istanbul, where the massive arcades of Justinian in St. Sophia have witnessed in turn Christian worship, Moslem prayers, and the emptiness of modern secularism; to Rome, Florence, and Ravenna, to Chartres and Rheims; to Durham,

Salisbury, and St. Paul's—to have made such a pilgrimage can only make one marvel at the legacy of grace and beauty which Christianity has bequeathed (should that be an appropriate word!) to the world. Of course buildings are not the Church. The Church managed for three hundred years without them, and if necessary could do so again. But Anglicans have always appreciated 'the holiness of beauty' as well as 'the beauty of holiness'. In the glorious buildings of Christendom, as well as in the humblest village churches, they have found 'God's presence near'. Most of those who love the Church, love its buildings too.

There is a liturgical heritage. *Lex orandi, lex credendi* is an old saying:—'what governs prayer, governs faith'. Beginning with the prayers of Jesus, and with 'the Lord's Prayer' which he taught, a stream of prayer comes down through Christian history. Much of it flows around the Holy Eucharist, a service which unites us with the very earliest days of the Church. Some of it is associated with music; if Gregory the Great returned to one of our churches there are chants and cadences which he could hear, and which would remind him of worship in Rome in the sixth century. Almost every age from that day to this has contributed *something* to the liturgical and musical tradition of Christian worship.

There is a scriptural tradition. If the English were once 'the people of a book', and that book the Bible, it is certain that the Bible is the book of a people, and that people the Church. Through the first one and half centuries after Christ, the New Testament was gradually taking shape. Books were being written, recognised as 'apostolic', and accepted into the 'official' Scriptures, the Canon. From the second century onwards those Greek books were being translated first into Syriac and Latin, and soon into other languages as well. The process has continued[1], and as I write this chapter England is all-agog with yet another translation, the New English Bible now fully completed, and proving a 'best-seller'. Who can estimate what this stream of holy writing and holy reading has meant to the Church down the ages, and in our own time? Without it we might know precious little of God's ancient people, of the story and teaching of Jesus, of the early history of the Church, and of what Christian faith means and implies. When I say 'I believe in the Church', one thing that I mean is that I value and treasure those writings which the Church has preserved for us—all through the Dark Ages when every syllable had to be written by hand and preserved in remote monasteries, until the day came when, by the invention of printing and the Reformation of church customs, 'the word of the Lord' could have free course, and sometimes, if not always, be glorified.

There is a doctrinal inheritance. Even in New Testament times we see the outlines of a primitive creed—as, for example, in I Corinthians 15. 3–8 in Philippians 2. 5–11; in Timothy 3. 16. In the second century this took the form of 'the Rule of Faith', soon to develop into the earliest Roman baptismal creed. This was not markedly different from our own Apostles' Creed. All down the centuries this faith has been held, taught and preached. Different ages have laid stress on different aspects of Christian faith—sometimes the Incarnation has been central, sometimes the Atonement: sometimes the Might and Majesty of the Creator, sometimes the innocence and humility of the Virgin Mother. But in one way and another, by preacher's voice or minstrel's carol, by village teacher and by university theologian, the faith of the Church has been preserved

[1] Some or all of the Bible has been translated into fourteen hundred languages.

until this day. If in our day we think we can purify and modernise it, let us at least be grateful for those who, in simple faith, have preserved it until now. Without their work and witness, there would be nothing to purify or modernise.

Finally, and in a sense including all that has gone before, there is an institutional heritage. For this faith, this worship, this tradition has been expressed and preserved by a complex of events which together make up the 'apostolic succession'. Some see in this mostly, or entirely, a succession in the apostles' doctrine: but some, including Anglicans, value also a succession in ministry, a ministry which by means of outward, tangible acts expresses its continuity with the ministry which our Lord first shared with his disciples, and then bestowed on his apostles. Most of us make no superstitious claim that an unbroken succession of ordination by laying-on-of-hands links us— as by an unbroken electric circuit—with the 'ordination' of the apostles, but the facts are sufficiently *near* to that to make the succession through episcopal ordination a precious sign that *our* ministry is Christ's Ministry. 'He that heareth you, heareth me' said Jesus to his disciples. We pray that this may be true in our ministry, and the sign and symbol of ordination, in historical continuity, encourages us to believe that our prayer may be answered.

When therefore we confess our belief (our *trust*) in the holy catholic Church what we are saying is that God has created the Church as an instrument whereby his gospel is made known, his name is hallowed, his kingdom enlarged, and in the bosom of which his sons and daughters are nurtured. Cyprian, in my view, was right when he said 'He cannot have God for his Father who has not the Church for his mother.' This is not a very popular saying nowadays, but is it not true? I have never known anyone

63

brought to a knowledge of God in Christ without the assistance *at some point*, of those who are Christians already. I have considered the evidence, of which there is quite a lot, that sometimes people have been 'converted' by the reading of scripture (e.g. a Gospel) without any human intervention. I find this evidence convincing, but I ask various questions about it. If Scripture is involved, does this not in itself implicate 'the Church'? Who wrote the New Testament Scriptures if not members of the Church? Who gave them canonical authority, and thus ensured their preservation? Who wrote and re-wrote the manuscripts? Who translated them? Who circulated them, and probably actually *gave* them to those who owe so much to them? And what would have happened to that new convert if there had been no other Christians, no Church, to welcome him, and give form and shape to the new resolve and decision?

The most radical critic of the Church himself *needs* the Church for his very existence. If he is judged critically and a little unkindly, he may be called a parasite *on* the Church—he derives his life from the Church he criticises. If he is judged charitably, he can be said to need *part* of the Church's tradition in order to establish his case against another part of it. He perhaps needs the Gospels in order to attack the Epistles (the authors of a recent book *Towards a radical church* do this very thing); he may need the prophets in order to attack the Law-books or the Wisdom literature; he may need St. Mark in order to criticise St. John; he may need the first century in order to expose, as he thinks, the errors of the fourth; he needs the establishment as a base from which to campaign for disestablishment.

For myself, far from finding 'I believe in the Church' the hardest clause of the Christian Creed, I find it the easiest. Of course like every sensible person I can see faults in the Church as it is, in my own, as well as in others. But what are these when contrasted with the immense blessings which the Church has brought me? 'I should not have believed in the Gospel', said St. Augustine, 'unless the authority of the Catholic Church had moved me to it.' The Church is (as I have said elsewhere) 'a school of faith, a home of love, a base for service, and a preparation for heaven' (*What's Right with the Church of England*, Lutterworth, 1967, p. 110). 'Christ loved the Church and gave Himself for it', so we are taught in Ephesians 5. 22. What Christ loved enough to die for, I must love enough to live for.

5

ONE BAPTISM — ONE BREAD

ONE BAPTISM

'I acknowledge one baptism for the remission of sins'—
these words come rather strangely in such an ancient and
august document as the Nicene Creed. When put alongside the tremendous statements about God and eternal
life they seem to strike an almost pedestrian note, dealing
as they do with just one of the Sacraments of the Church.
At one moment the thought is of the two eternities
between which all history seems to occupy but a fleeting
moment: at the next, one is at the font for a christening,
an event which does not always succeed in holding its
own (in popular esteem) against the family party which is
to follow. We shall have to look at these words and
enquire what they are doing in the Creed. Having done
so, it will give us an opportunity to consider the phrase
which we have bracketed with 'One baptism', viz. 'One
Bread'. We shall then have at least glanced at what it
means to believe not only in 'the Word', the message, but
also in the Sacraments.

Any form of Catholic (or 'mainstream') Christianity
must base itself on the *two* foundations, Word and Sacrament. This is clearly stated in Article 19 of the Church of
England: 'The visible Church of Christ is a congregation
of faithful men, in which the pure Word of God is
preached, and the Sacraments duly administered according to Christ's ordinance . . ..' These words echo fairly
closely those of the Augsburg Confession of 1530, which

has been the framework for Lutheran theology ever since: 'This Church (i.e. 'the one Holy Church') will remain for ever. Now this Church is the congregation of the saints, in which the Gospel is rightly taught and the Sacraments rightly administered.' The pre-Reformation Roman Catholic Church lacked clear statements balancing Word and Sacrament in this way, but it may be noted that it was that Church which had preserved *the letter* of Holy Scripture—without that Luther could not have come under the spell of Scripture as a saving word—and its stress on the Sacraments was so great as to be, if anything, excessive. So it is not really surprising to find a reference to at least one Sacrament in the Creed. Baptism is a door to the whole life of the Christian and of the Church, and the reference to it gives the whole sacramental system a firm place in the declaration of our basic faith.

There was a time in the history of the Church when the reference to baptism in the Creed was even more striking than it is now. The Creed given in the so-called *Apostolic Constitutions* begins with the words, 'I believe *and am baptised* into One, unbegotten, only true God'. It continues 'and into the Lord Jesus Christ . . . and I am baptised also into the Holy Ghost' (then follow the usual phrases about the Church, the forgiveness of sins and eternal life). So one might say, that judged by that standard, the strange thing is not the insertion of 'I acknowledge one baptism for the remission of sins' but the *omission* of the reference to baptism at the beginning of the other main sections. At least all this reminds us that the Creeds are fundamentally *baptismal* documents. They state the faith in which, and into which, we are baptised. Their regular repetition (as e.g. at the Holy Communion) is a way of re-asserting our baptismal *stance*, a way of re-constituting the baptised community. It is interesting to note that before 'The Peace' in the Series II Communion Service, the words are said 'We are the Body of Christ. By one Spirit we were baptised into one Body'. This makes the importance of baptism as the foundation of the Eucharistic community even plainer than before.

The first written evidence for the phrase 'one baptism for the remission of sins' is to be found in a writing of Epiphanius (315–403 Bishop of Salamis, and Metropolitan of Cyprus) dated A.D. 374. There is some doubt, however, as to whether the text of the Creed given in the manuscript has not been 'doctored' to make it match exactly the Creed known in our Prayer Book as Nicene, but which is actually an expansion of the original Nicene Creed (A.D. 325) finally approved at the Council of Chalcedon (A.D. 451) but stated at that Council to have been authorised at the Council of Constantinople (A.D. 381).

For our purposes all we need to note is that the phrase 'One baptism for the remission of sins' has been part of the Creed since the later part of the Fourth Century. Before that St. Cyril of Jerusalem in the middle years of that century had included in his baptismal instruction the phrase 'one baptism *of repentance* for the remission of sins'.

What was the origin of this phrase, in its slightly variant forms? It probably has a double history. Many of the other clauses have the numerical 'one' attached to them ('One God', 'One Lord Jesus Christ', 'One Holy, Catholic, Apostolic Church') so it was not surprising that where there was any kind of appropriateness they should insert the word 'one' lower down, as they did in the phrase 'one baptism for the remission of sins'. But there was a scriptural precedent too, the famous words of Ephesians 4. 4–6: 'There is one body, and one Spirit, even as also ye were called in one hope of your calling; one Lord, one faith, one baptism, one God, and Father of all, who is over all, and through all, and in all.' I have shown elsewhere (New Testament Studies Vol. I, No. I, September 1954, *Logic verses Experience in the Order of Credal Formulae*) that these words do in fact present a kind of Creed, with the items in almost the reverse order to that followed in our Creeds. Here the start is from the Church and the Spirit, and the climax is the reference to the all-creative and all-sustaining God. But that is by the way. The point is that here we have a string of 'ones' including 'one baptism'. This passage may well have influenced the form in which the Creed took its shape.

Once it was there, what did it mean? What has it come to mean?

It first recognised a basic fact about Christianity— Baptism was the only way in. It could virtually be said that until the coming into history of the Quakers, and later of the Salvation Army, there never were any Christians claiming the name who had entered the Christian Church (even divided parts of it) in any other way than by being baptised with water in the name of the Holy Trinity. Certainly the New Testament knows of no such anomaly. When Cornelius appeared to be given the gift of the Holy Spirit before baptism St. Peter deduced that Baptism must immediately follow (Acts 10. 47: 'Can any man forbid water, that these should not be baptised, which have received the Holy Ghost as well as we?') Acts shows Baptism to be the invariable gateway into the life of the Christian Church. In the Epistles we have earlier written evidence of the universality of baptism (*see*, e.g. Galatians 3. 27: 'As many of you as were baptised into Christ did put on Christ'). The Epistle to the Romans develops the theme, and here there is great stress on the significance of baptism as a dying with Christ in his death, and a rising to new life with him in his Resurrection (*see especially* Romans 6. 3–4).

But of course the most important thing is not whether baptism was in fact universal as a means of entry into Christianity, but whether this was so because of 'Christ's Ordinance'. Certainly the Gospels assume that this was so. St. Matthew ends with a clear command (St. Matthew 28. 19: 'Go ye therefore and make disciples of all the nations, baptising them into the name of the Father and the Son and the Holy Ghost.') Most scholars think that this very developed Trinitarian formula suggests that the words date from a time much later than the immediate post-Resurrection period. This might of course apply to the formula but not to the command, but once the point has been raised it is difficult to rely entirely on that one verse. St. Mark (*see* St. Mark 16. 16) has a similar command (without the formula) in 'the later postscript', but this appears to be a repeat of what is in St. Matthew. St. Luke tells us nothing of the command in the Gospel, but Acts, also from his pen, shows his belief that baptism was basic. St. John has the one impressive statement (St. John 3. 5) 'Except a man be born of water and the spirit he cannot enter the kingdom of God'. There is also a cryptic reference to baptism carried out by the disciples of Jesus during his lifetime in St. John 4. 2. It should be remembered that all the Gospels tell us of the work of John the Baptist as the introduction to the Gospel story and it could be that here is the clearest evidence that Christian baptism was in line with the will of Christ. Jesus himself was baptised (this raised strange questions in the minds of early Christians, one of which St. Matthew tried to answer: St. Matthew 3. 14–15) and it seems that the Christian movement was felt, by the Evangelists at least, to be in direct succession to that 'baptism of repentance' which John the

Baptist initiated. That is one reason why the phrase 'remission of sins' is associated with Christian baptism from the start. Compare Luke 3. 3 and Acts 2. 38 for a picture of how St. Luke saw the continuity between the two rites. The need was the same—remission of sins. The condition was the same—repentance. The occasion was different—for now Christ had died and risen again. Now all had to be done 'in the name of Jesus Christ', and those who were so baptised were promised the gift of the Holy Spirit.

Why God should have attached importance to an outward act it is not for us to say. Perhaps one reason is that by this means all stand on the same ground. There are endless differences between Christians—differences of cleverness, wealth, age, sex, class, race, and disposition, but there is *one* baptism for the remission of sins.

The word *one* can of course carry a double meaning. It *can* mean 'once only for each person' and the Church does in fact act as though that was at least one of its meanings. We do not repeat baptism, wherever and whenever it has been given, so long as it has been done with water and with the invocation of the name of the Trinity. There is only one door into the sheepfold, and, sacramentally speaking, once you are in, you cannot get out! 'None shall pluck them out of my hand.'

But there is a deeper meaning in 'one baptism' than a mere injunction not to repeat it. When we say 'I acknowledge one baptism for the remission of sins' we are saying something very important about Christian unity. We are saying that there is only one real Church of Christ, and all the baptised make up its members. This has never been more strikingly put, and never with greater historical significance, than by Vatican II. In the 'Constitution' on Ecumenism we read, 'By the sacrament of baptism,

71

whenever it is properly conferred in the way the Lord determined, and received with the appropriate dispositions of soul, a man becomes truly incorporated into the crucified and glorified Christ and is reborn to a sharing of the divine life, as the apostle says: "For you were buried together with him in baptism, and in him also rose again through faith in the working of God who raised him from the dead".' (Colossians 2. 12; cf. Romans 6. 4) 'Baptism' (the Council continued) 'therefore constitutes a sacramental bond of unity linking all who have been reborn by means of it.' (*Documents of Vatican I*, Abbott and Gallacher. Geoffrey Chapman, 1966, pp. 362–3).

Allowance has to be made for a special idiom current in the Roman Catholic Church, and for the fact that the words given are translated from the Latin. The meaning, however, comes through, and it is just what Anglicans believe.

To give reality to the whole phrase of the Creed, we must add a word about 'remission of sins'. I suspect that these words, repeated so often, mean very little to many of our people. Can they be made to mean more? I think they can.

Even in Holy Scripture, questions of sin and forgiveness do not *exhaust* the relationships which exist or arise between man and God. There is the relation of creature to Creator; of child to Father; of worshipper to the All-Holy —and so on. But there is no doubt that the Christian religion moves very much within a sphere in which God's moral demands, and his grace in forgiving our failures and enabling our efforts are extremely important. The Cross, which stands supreme in Scripture, in liturgy, in symbolism, in the Calendar, and in theology, proves this. Yet I suspect that many find it hard to think realistically about 'remission of sins' in connection with baptism, especially when it is administered in infancy as it is with us. So can we think of it like this? Christian life is life lived in reconciled fellowship with God, life lived as a child with his Father, life lived in a forgiven and forgiving family, life where God 'breaks the power of cancelled sin'. Into this realm, baptism admits. As it confers the blessings of the new life, it confers also the demands. God's message, and God's action in baptism is a message and action both of demand and of succour. When we 'confess' our baptism, we rejoice that our sins have been and will be forgiven. We rejoice that we know what it is to be forgiven by our friends, and to forgive them. Of all this, what symbol could be more fitting than 'the washing of our bodies with pure water'. We may not remember it, any more than we remember our natural birth, but we know that we have passed from death unto life. And we acknowledge one baptism, our own and others, 'for the remission of sins'.

When Martin Luther was depressed, and tempted of the Devil, he used to write on his pad 'Baptizatus sum'—'I have been baptised'. Would that our baptism meant more to us. It is partly the fault of us clergy that it does not. For in spite of endless arguments about the meaning of baptism, about its conditions and effectiveness, how often does an ordinary Christian, in an ordinary service, hear a simple explanation of its meaning, or a reminder of its power?

ONE BREAD

We now turn to the second section of this chapter. This we have entitled 'One Bread'. Of course there is no such phrase or subject in the Creed, and we may wonder why[1]. One explanation might be that most of the clauses in the Creed reflected some kind of contemporary conflict or difficulty—something that called for a clear stand by the

[1] Unless 'Communion of Saints' is a mistranslation, and should read 'Communion in holy things', i.e. in the Sacraments, which is quite possible.

Church. It is an interesting fact, perhaps to our modern minds a surprising one, that the Eucharist, centre of so many discussions for the last four hundred years, was not a particular centre of controversy in the early centuries. It is true that some non-Christians occasionally pointed to it as a mysterious secret rite with some cannibalistic aspect about it (the language about 'eating the flesh' and 'drinking the blood' could easily be brought in to support such charges) but within the Church the Eucharist was just accepted as the main, if not sometimes the only regular service for the whole Church. To accept the 'One Baptism' therefore, was to enter into the fellowship of the 'One Bread' and for some reason the early Christians did not think it necessary to say so explicitly. There may even have been some reluctance to lay open to all and sundry mysteries which were only properly understood and reverenced within the Christian community. It is of course an obvious fact that in the sixteenth century, when the nature of the Holy Communion began to be a subject of controversy, the churches then dividing began to explain fully the particular view-point they held in this matter (e.g. the Prayer Book Catechism and Articles 25, 28, 29, 30, and 31).

The Eucharist then is not neglected or underrated in the Creeds; it is taken for granted, understood, and assumed.

Nevertheless, it is always a useful exercise to go back over the early evidence and to see how very central the Eucharist is to the life and worship of the first Christians. We can begin with St. Paul, and note that the very earliest written references to the Eucharist are in his first letter to the Corinthians, written about A.D. 55. Here are two very important references, the first in I Corinthians 10. 14–22, the second in I Corinthians 11. 19–34.

The first is a short description of what the Communion is, and it is very significant that the opening words of the section have been chosen to be said at the very heart of the new Communion Service known as Series II: 'The cup of blessing, which we bless, is it not a sharing of the blood of Christ? The bread which we break, is it not a sharing of the body of Christ? Seeing that we, who are many, are one bread, one body: for we all partake of the one bread.' Whether St. Paul intended to emphasise the word 'all' to indicate the universality (among Christians) of eucharistic participation, his words can certainly be taken by us as a reminder of a well-known fact. The *contemporary* meaning of St. Paul's words for us is something to which we can and must return later.

The second passage is extremely interesting, and the two have to be read together if, once more, a vivid stereoscopic image is to be obtained. For if the first showed what the Communion essentially *was*, the second showed how it was related to history. St. Paul regrets that owing to the selfish and greedy habits of some of the Corinthian Church it was 'not possible' for them to eat 'the Lord's supper' (I Corinthians 11. 20). This is clearly what they were *supposed* to be doing, perhaps even what they *wanted* to do, but to be a real 'Lord's supper' a certain attitude of mutual love and consideration was prerequisite. The reason for this was that the origin of the whole 'ceremony' (we use this word, though there was clearly none in our modern sense of the word) was what the Lord Jesus did 'in the night in which he was betrayed' (verse 23). Then, we are told, he took bread, gave thanks, broke it, and gave it to his disciples, saying 'This is my body, which is broken, given for you (possibly just 'for you' as in Revised Version). This do in remembrance of me.' Likewise with the cup, which Jesus is said to describe as 'the new covenant in my blood'. In this way the disciples were to 'shew forth' his death till he came again (verse 26). So the sharing of the body of Christ, and of his Blood (as mentioned in I Corinthians 10) was a sharing in a Body and a Blood which was full of sacred memories, but memories not confined to past history. They were memories which incorporated the present 'rememberers' into a contemporary organic unity with each other, because all were being united with a Christ who had died, had risen, was to come, but was all the time with his people. There is no reason to think that St. Paul's words represented a peculiar or a provincial point of view. They accord very well with the rest of the New Testament, although it is not necessary to believe that the story of the Last Supper was the *sole* source of that stream of eucharistic life that flowed into the early Church. It may well have been enriched by memories of hill-side feedings in Galilee, and we are shown in Acts that memories of post-Easter meals and picnics were vividly retained in the early days of missionary activity (*see* Acts 10. 40–41).

Having looked at the earliest available *written* evidence it is time to look at the *next* earliest, and that is the evidence of the Gospels. It is never easy for non-specialists to remember that as *documents* the Gospels come after the Epistles, although the facts they record are of course earlier in time than the appearance of the Epistles. Moreover the Gospels did not suddenly appear 'out of the blue' from A.D. 65 onwards. Parts of them must have existed almost from the start, either as verbal memories or as short stories and sayings later to be built up into continuous documents, like 'Q' (a name often given to a 'sayings' tradition), or Mark. The accounts of the Last Supper in St. Mark, St. Matthew, and St. Luke do not differ so very much from the Pauline account in I Corinthians 11, although microscopic examination by scholars does reveal a certain 'speciality' about all of them. Thus St. Luke alone has a 'do this' clause, and that in what is called his 'longer text', a text which leaves him with two cups. St. Mark makes our Lord say over the cup 'This is my blood of the covenant', instead of 'This cup is the new covenant in my blood'. Some scholars detect in Mark's version a growing emphasis on the actual *contents* of the cup, as apart from a symbolism attached to the sharing of the cup itself, and hence think that the Marcan version is later. If, as is commonly thought, Mark originated in Rome about A.D. 65, a coherent picture would be emerging. But for eighteen hundred years and more Christians lived with the Gospel and the Pauline accounts side by side and found no great difficulties. It is only modern scholars who have to listen to the New Testament evidence so carefully that they 'can hear the grass grow' who have found the subtle differences between them.

Acts is probably to be dated soon after Luke, and throws a little light on what its author thought to have happened in the early days. Here we find that the 'breaking of bread' took its place alongside loyalty to 'the apostles' teaching and fellowship' and to continuing steadfastly in 'the prayers' (Acts 2. 42). Acts 20 gives us a priceless vignette of a midnight 'bread-breaking' at Troas, which shows, among other things, that this took place on the first day of the week.

The Fourth Gospel, which we saw took its own special line in the matter of our Lord's divinity, takes its own line also in the matter of the Eucharist. To begin with there is no actual account of anything like an 'institution' of the Lord's Supper. Instead we have some deep teaching about 'eating Christ's flesh' and 'drinking his blood' in chapter 6, following the feeding of the five thousand. This shows that these conceptions stood in the forefront of the mind of the writer of the Gospel, and it seems to point to an attitude halfway to that of Ignatius who, in A.D. 106, is talking about 'the food of immortality'. To have eternal life, says St. John, it is necessary to 'eat the flesh' and 'drink the blood'. But alongside this strongly sacramental language lies a saying like John 6. 63: 'It is the spirit that quickeneth; the flesh profiteth nothing; the words that I have spoken unto you, they are spirit and they are life.' It is not easy to say whether this passage is meant to be something of a counterweight to the strongly sacramental language that precedes it, or whether it just is there to give a moral and spiritual content to sacramental language wholeheartedly accepted.

The next important evidence about the place of the Eucharist in the Early Church comes from the writings of the Fathers of the Church, men like Justin Martyr (A.D. 150), Hippolytus (A.D. 200), St. Cyril of Jerusalem (A.D. 350), St. Chrysostom (A.D. 400), and St. Augustine (A.D. 400). These are just typical figures whose writings give us clear pictures either of the kind of service which was held, or of the meaning attached to it. In varying forms, revealing a great similarity between the various Eastern liturgies, and a similar family likeness among the Western forms, the Eucharist came down from the Patristic Age into the Middle Ages. In the West, which concerns us most directly, 'the Mass' completely dominated the liturgical scene. It was celebrated every day by every priest, and the Sunday Parish Mass occupied much the same place as it holds today in Catholic Churches on the Continent (and indeed in our country too).

After the Reformation the pattern varied a good deal. There was a reaction against what had come to seem (and I should think really was) a very superstitious attitude to the Mass, both as to its effectiveness as a sacrifice 'for the living and the dead', and as to the effects of 'Transubstantiation' (the medieval theory used to explain the effects of consecration on the bread and the wine). There was also a quite new (or very much revived) interest in 'the Word'—the Word read, in its new vernacular versions, and the Word preached. Time had to be found for this new aspect of worship, and although some leading Reformers, like John Calvin, always hoped for weekly celebrations of the Holy Communion, they in fact became rarer. The Church of England closed for 'three times in the year' as the absolute minimum observance for each communicant, and sometimes church practice came down to meet the minimum requirement, i.e. there were only three or four celebrations a year.

In theory the church stood for weekly celebrations, and provided prayers and readings in the Prayer Book accordingly, but in this matter practice rarely kept up with theory. By Victorian times, the normal custom was a stately Matins each Sunday, Evensong either in the afternoon or evening, and Holy Communion after Matins for those who wished to 'stay behind' as the saying went. The Oxford Movement set in train a marked sacramental revival and churches strongly influenced by that movement had a weekly, and sometimes a daily celebration.

In our day we have seen a virtually universal 'Early Celebration' weekly, but the last twenty years have seen an increasingly widespread use of a 'Parish Communion', weekly, *after* breakfast, usually about 10 a.m.

The 'One Bread' has been taken in many forms, but it has never quite ceased to be used and reverenced. Apart from Quakers and Salvationists, Christians of every kind, in every land, in every century have 'partaken of the one Bread'. At an infinite variety of altars and tables,

Christians of all kinds have 'eaten and worshipped'.

The question now arises: What does 'the one Bread' mean to us to-day? We should, I think, admit that different ages, different cultures, have seen different 'values' in the Eucharist. I will not pause to describe all the past variants, but will come at once to those insights which make a special appeal to-day, and not only to Christians in our own Church. It is a striking fact that there is a wide area of agreement between Anglican and Roman Catholic theologians at the present time, as well of course as considerable areas of disagreement. 'They get more and more like us every day' the Pope is *supposed* to have said when he saw our Series II! This story is probably apocryphal, but it need not have been. Most of the items in the service which had been arranged in a distinctively 'Reformation' order at the Reformation are restored, either compulsorily or voluntarily, to their pre-Reformation (hence modern Roman) position in Series II. And this has been done with widespread, if not unanimous approval in the Church of England. I mention this now only as an illustration of the fact that the same waves of liturgical thought are washing over the Church of England as are washing over the Vatican!

What do these waves convey? They convey a firm belief that the Eucharist is primarily a corporate not an individual act. It is an act of the Church. Of course participation in it is an individual duty and an individual privilege, but the idea of the service going on 'up there in the sanctuary' while the individual Christian says his own prayers is 'out' as a principle, whether we are thinking of an Anglican 'Early Service' or a Roman 'Low Mass'. This is not to say that for many years opportunities will not be given to those who have learned to worship in this way, but it can no longer control and motivate developments.

The corporate act is an act by means of which the local church is re-formed, refreshed, and re-nourished. The Church, which *is* 'One Body', becomes, in a new and lively sense 'One Body', by partaking of 'the One Bread'. Partaking of that 'One Bread' is a sharing in a memory—that of the One Sacrifice on Calvary, with all that led up to it, and all that followed it—and a sharing in a present experience of worship, thanksgiving, intercession, and resolve. One picture which I have found helpful is this: Christ at the Last Supper inaugurated, though necessarily in a preliminary way, the sacrament of Holy Communion: ever since, the circle of his disciples, thus gathered round him, has been enlarged, and is still enlarging. We have our chance to take our place in the circle, thus bringing forward, to a tiny degree, the day when the circle will be complete, when Christ shall have 'completed the number of his elect' as we anticipate in the Funeral Service of the Church.

To the individual participant, and to the Church, the living Christ comes, true to his promise to meet even the two or three gathered in his name. He comes both with his gifts and his call—his gifts of forgiveness, compassion, hope and strength; his call to closer discipleship, fuller dedication, wider and deeper compassion for the lonely and the lost. But this emphasis on the earthly community, brought into living union with Christ the Saviour, does not *exhaust* the meaning of the 'One Bread'. For Christians can never finally exclude from the Eucharist thoughts which revolve around the idea of sacrifice. Christians agree that Our Lord's death was *in some sense* a sacrifice for sin. All biblically-minded Christians recognise that *in some sense* Christ, the true High Priest, presents himself eternally before his Father as 'the propitiation for our sins'. All agree that the Eucharist brings these thoughts vividly before our minds. Can we go further, and say that 'our sacrifice of praise and thanksgiving' is part of, or is linked with, the eternal sacrifice of Christ. William Bright's hymn, 'And now, O Father, mindful of the love', has sung its way into the hearts of Anglican Eucharistic worshippers over a hundred years, and much of the Protestant objection to some of its lines has been melted by the combined effect of corporate devotion and Victorian music. When it came to the point of finding an expression of this for use by all Anglicans in Series II, the following formula was finally agreed upon by an enormous majority: 'Wherefore, O Lord, with this bread, and with this cup, we make the memorial of his saving passion, his resurrection from the dead and his glorious ascension into heaven and we look for the coming of his kingdom. We pray thee to accept this our duty and service and grant that we may so eat and drink these holy things, in the presence of Thy divine majesty, that we may be filled with thy grace and heavenly blessing'. That represents both the lowest common denominator, and the highest common factor, of Anglican thought on the Eucharistic sacrifice.

To some extent the shift of emphasis from the individual communicant, individually receiving the consecrated elements, to an emphasis on the whole church, partaking in the whole cycle of Eucharistic acts, has placed all the traditional controversies in a new perspective and a new light. Thus although there has been no withdrawal from the traditional Anglican view that consecration of the elements *does* something (however widely the idea of what it does may vary) it is clear that if the stress is now on the *whole* Eucharistic action, the location in time of the moment of consecration is more difficult to specify. Once the location *in time* of the moment of consecration becomes a matter of discussion, questions of location *in space* of the divine presence become more arguable. On the other hand, once reservation for the sick has been accepted (as it now is almost throughout the Church of England) reservation *between* sick communions becomes inevitable, and manners and methods cannot be excluded from discussion by a hasty resort to Article 28, where we learn, quite rightly, that the Sacrament 'was not by Christ's ordinance reserved, carried about, lifted up or worshipped'.

This is not to say that all disputed questions can now be quietly pigeon-holed as 'irrelevant' or 'unanswerable'. There are still questions which affect practice, and which still have to be solved.

Does it matter who celebrates? Our Church still believes that as the Eucharist is an act of the Church (or perhaps an act of the Lord *in* his Church) its *ecclesial* character should be marked, and this is best done by the minister carrying the authority of the Church by means of episcopal ordination. Until recently many (but not all) Anglicans thought that this meant (1) very severe restrictions on non-Anglicans being admitted to our altars, (2) complete abstention by Anglicans from participation at Free Church communions. I can only say that today both these views are subject to strong criticism, indeed erosion, under the pressure of oecumenical developments. Many— and I must count myself among them—would say that the incomplete, but definite, unity of all Christians through their baptism, allows of some intercommunion, including reciprocal intercommunion. Equally we should feel that as the final union of all Christians is clearly still in the eschatological future, some restraint is necessary, so that sacramental unity may go alongside of growing organic unity, and not be quite severed from it. 'Already, but not yet' is a phrase that applies both to our Christian possessions, and to our Christian policy.

83

One small practical question is still troublesome. The widespread revival, so welcome, of 'parish communion' as the chief Sunday Service, is something of an embarrassment when a wider community, accustomed to occasional attendance at the parish church (on Easter morning, for instance) finds that it is a case of 'all or nothing'— Eucharist, or stay away! There is no easy answer to this question. Perhaps the Eucharist can be so conducted that 'the wayfaring man may not err therein' or perhaps a more general service can be fitted in, before or after the Eucharist, to accommodate our modern 'catechumenate' —which may include some 90 per cent of the population.

The meaning and significance of the Holy Communion is influenced by the same tendencies in thought as are influencing the doctrines of God and of Christ. In these, there is a strong tendency to concentrate on dynamic rather than on static ideas. Thus there is a retreat from thoughts of God as the Unchangeable, the Unmoved Mover (although we have seen that such ideas still have their value) and a move towards God as involved in the massive movements of nature and history. There is a retreat from the thought of 'the two natures' in Christ (though this idea safeguards some truths still necessary to right thinking) and a move towards attention to what God was *doing* in Christ, towards measuring Christ's uniqueness by the uniqueness of what God was doing in him and through him. Similarly, there is a retreat from undue concentration on the elements of bread and wine as 'things in themselves', even when consecrated to 'be unto us the Body and Blood of the Lord', and a move towards concentration on what *happens* when the bread and wine are used in the way the Lord commanded. It is significant that the text chosen as the 'theme song' of Series II is 'We being many are one Body, for we all *partake* of the one Bread.'

84

This is not the old-fashioned kind of 'receptionism' where the stress was on the individual 'feeding upon Christ', but a kind of 'objective, corporate receptionism' where the corporate act is used by God to bring about a new and re-invigorated 'Body of Christ', both in the Church and in the world.

6

LIFE ETERNAL—
Here and Hereafter (1)

THE ABSOLUTION, in the new Communion Service, ends with the words 'and keep you in life eternal'. This replaces the words in the old Service 'and bring you to everlasting life'. If the change implied that there is no longer any confidence in the life everlasting it would be wholly deplorable but of course that is not the case. It is true that the word 'everlasting' is open to some objection, as it can be taken to mean an endless succession in time of a life in sequence to our life here and now, and however little we know about the life beyond we can be pretty certain that it is not to be measured by the standards of earthly time. On the other hand 'life eternal' is not as different from 'life everlasting' as some might think, for the English phrase usually translates a Greek one meaning 'the life of the aeons'. Undoubtedly there is a time element in the meaning of 'life eternal' but it is not *only* a description of life going on for ever. 'The ages' stand in contrast to this age, and 'eternal life' can mean life of a certain quality, life which certainly transcends the limitations of time, and is not terminable by human mortality, but a life which certainly can begin now, and is known in part by all those who have 'tasted the good word of God and the powers of the age to come' (Hebrews 6. 5). One of the most well-known uses of the phrase is in the 'great High Priestly prayer' of St. John 17, where in verse 3 Our Lord says 'This is eternal life, to know God, and Jesus Christ whom

He hath sent'. On any showing Christians *begin* to know God, and Christ his Son, here and now, so it must be right to think of eternal life beginning here and now. Thus it is assumed in the eucharistic absolution that those present have in some sense 'passed from death unto life', by baptism, confirmation and conversion, so the prayer is made, not that they may one day be brought to everlasting life, but that they may be kept 'in life eternal'.

If we revert to the language of the Creeds we find a variety of uses. The Apostles' Creed ends: 'the Resurrection of the body and the Life everlasting'. The Nicene Creed uses rather more sophisticated language, and language that sits rather more easily on modern lips: 'I look for the Resurrection of the dead, and the Life of the world to come'. There is little doubt that both Creeds are referring to the same thing—what we call 'the after-life', and we shall return to that subject in the last half of the next chapter. We must note in passing, however, that in both creeds these thoughts of the after-life are linked with a group of ideas at first sight only distantly related to them. The Apostles' Creed attaches to 'belief in the Holy Ghost' an expression of belief in 'the communion of saints, the forgiveness of sins, the resurrection of the body, and the life everlasting'. In other words faith in the Holy Spirit is not treated as an isolated belief, but as a belief which introduces the believer to *a life*, a life characterised by a sharing with others in holy things (e.g. sacraments, prayer, witness and worship). It is a life in which sins can be forgiven by God, and must be forgiven among ourselves. It is a life marked by a confident hope of resurrection to eternal life. It was an easy step for the early Christians to take when in the Nicene Creed they described the Holy Ghost as Lord, and as 'Giver of life'. In that Creed they lingered to put in some controversial detail about the Holy

Spirit—that he proceeded from the Father *and* the Son, that he spoke by the Prophets, that he was entitled to the same worship as the Father and the Son; but they then moved on to the phrase we have already considered, 'One baptism for the remission of sins', which means that baptism is baptism into a forgiven and forgiving life, and then straight into a confession of faith in the resurrection of the dead, and the life of the world to come. The point I am making is this: belief in the Spirit is belief in a whole complex of experiences, two of the most important of which are forgiveness now and eternal life hereafter. In between lie those experiences which are summed up in the phrase 'the communion of saints' which can include our communion with all God's people living and departed, but which principally means the sharing in holy *things* (taking *communio sanctorum* as meaning *communio in sacris*).

I hope it will now be clear why I have chosen the title *Life eternal, here and hereafter* to cover the last two chapters of this book. I certainly want to say something, before it closes, about the life beyond, but I want to suggest that eternal life begins here, and is another way of describing 'the life that is life indeed', that 'new life' to which we are called to rise in our baptism, that new life with the risen Christ to which every Easter invites us (*see* Colossians 3. 1, the Epistle for Easter Day) and to which we were called in 'the Invitation' of the old Communion: 'Ye that do truly and earnestly repent you of your sins, and are in love and charity with your neighbours, and intend to lead *a new life*'—perhaps it would always have been better to say '*the new life*'. There was always something slightly unreal about a call to lead 'a new life' sounding out every Sunday, or even every day. Such a completely 'renewed' conversion could hardly be expected, but the call to rise to the heights of '*the* new life', always beyond what we have

88

so far achieved, could be always relevant and always challenging.

We shall now turn our attention to a number of features of 'the new life', that 'eternal life here' to which we have been introduced by our baptism, in which we have been confirmed, and which has been continually renewed in us, and we in it, as Sunday by Sunday we have been laid hold of by Christ and have again laid hold on him in the Holy Communion of his Body and his Blood.

First a word about 'the new life' and 'the old life'.

The first of the four short prayers in the 1662 Prayer Book service for the baptism of infants reads: 'O merciful God, grant that the old Adam in this child may be so buried, that the new man may be raised up in him'. The contrast here is between 'the old Adam' and 'the new man'. It must have mystified many generations of non-theologically minded church people! The prayer itself represented a rather telescoped version of some closely related, but distinct ideas to be found in the Pauline literature. In I Corinthians 15 St. Paul draws a contrast between Adam and Christ. 'The first man Adam' (verse 45) was 'a living soul' but 'the last Adam' became 'a life-giving spirit (impossible to say whether the 'S' should be capital or not). We have 'borne the image of the earthly' (i.e. we know our solidarity with the genus 'man', ordinary humanity); we shall bear the image of the heavenly (i.e. be made like Christ). In Romans 6 St. Paul speaks of 'our old man' (verse 6) being crucified with Christ, and of our hope of being 'raised with him' to newness of life. This passage occurs in the course of a treatment of what 'baptism into Christ' (verse 3) really means. In Ephesians 4. 22–4 there is a direct contrast between 'the old man' which has to be put off, like a garment, and 'the new man' which has to be put on, also like a garment. So it is that progress in

89

the Christian life is described in the prayer as the burying of 'the old Adam' and the raising up of 'the new man'.

There are certain ways in which this imagery is undoubtedly appropriate. It is a fundamental truth that Christ has brought into human history 'a new humanity', and hat he invites all men to be linked with him in it—he is to be 'the firstborn among many brethren' (Romans 8. 29). It is true that the Fourth Gospel speaks of the necessity of the new birth—'Ye must be born again' says Our Lord to Nicodemus (St. John 3. 7). It is true that, if any man be in Christ he is (or there is) a new creation. It is true that when there is a very sharp distinction between a way of life followed *before* faith in Christ, and the way of life followed *after* coming to believe in him, language about 'the old life' and 'the new life' has an obvious appropriateness. This may be true of an individual experiencing a definite conversion, or of a tribe or nation coming for the first time under the sound of the Gospel. It is possible to see a whole human life as a struggle between a lower and a higher nature, sometimes expressed in shorthand as the conflict of 'flesh' and 'spirit'. But when everything has been said some of us feel that the language is not very apt as a description of how Christianity affects normal people in normal times. It is particularly hard to feel that a prayer for the 'burial of the old Adam' is a natural prayer to make in connection with an unconscious baby. Theologians may understand it, but ordinary people do not.

Is it not true that such excessive *polarisation* between 'the old life' and 'the new life' fails to express the kind of spiritual pilgrimage which most Christians feel themselves to be engaged upon? Surely an obvious fact is that all human beings, Christian or not, share a common heritage of manhood. This manhood has as its base the physical, even the animal constitution given to us at birth. Regardless of man's spiritual possibilities, the life-cycle of birth, growth, play, work, mating, reproduction, maturity, old age, and death are shared (more or less) by all. This is life, human life, and all are given it and called to enjoy it. Christians, however, believe that in it and through it they are called to share in life at a new depth, life with a new dimension added to it.

This dimension is that of 'new life in Christ'. By the sacramental gateway of baptism and confirmation, by growth into personal discipleship of Christ, by training and discipline in Church life, the Christian becomes aware of realities not observed or cared for by those without this dimension. The realities include the possibility of fellow-ship with God in prayer; the sense that God calls us to share with him in establishing his reign or kingdom, not in any final sense, but in successive places and situations; a sense of union with Our Lord both as recipients of 'the benefits of his Passion' and as those who share with him such burdens of suffering or sorrow that we meet, either our own or those of others; the sense of resurrection in and through suffering because we are united to the Risen One; a sense of fellowship with those who share our inheritance in Christ; and a sense that life is not bounded by the horizons of this world, but extends into the unseen and the unknown; a deep hope for the future, based on the sense that since Christ lives, we shall live with him. Words are poor instruments to describe such profound and penetrating experiences, and not all Christians have them all, or all the time. But Christians recognise what is being talked about when these things are said. Every preacher knows what it means to 'strike a chord' in the hearts of his hearers. Then he knows that 'deep answers unto deep'. The writer of the Johannine Epistles has many phrases in which he sums up this kind of experience, none terser than when he says in I John 5. 12, 'He that hath the Son hath the life'. 'Having the Son' means coming into the experience of possessing, and being possessed by Christ the Son, Christ the Word once made flesh. Through him we have 'access to the Father', through him we say, as he did, in trust and obedience, 'Abba, Father'.

It will, I hope, be profitable to look in turn at a number of characteristic features of 'the new life', and we can begin by thinking about the important subject of prayer.

PRAYER

Rather than beginning to write about prayer as though no one had done so before I propose to start from a hymn about the subject that used to be well known in certain circles, but which is rarely heard now: I do not think I have heard it sung during my sixteen years as Bishop of Leicester. It is James Montgomery's 'Prayer is the soul's sincere desire'. Montgomery was an interesting character. He was born in 1771 and died in 1854. His father was a Moravian Minister; he became an accomplished and courageous journalist, editing *The Sheffield Iris* for thirty-one years, and being twice imprisoned for technical offences. The *Dictionary of Hymnology* writes thus of his gifts as poet and hymn-writer: 'The secrets of his power as a writer of hymns were manifold. His poetic genius was of a high order, higher than most who stand with him in the front rank of Christian poets. His ear for rhythm was exceedingly accurate and refined. His knowledge of Holy Scripture was most extensive. His religious views were broad and charitable. His devotional spirit was of the holiest type. With the faith of a strong man he united the beauty and simplicity of a child' (op. cit. p. 764). Among his other well-known hymns are 'Angels from the realms of glory' and 'For ever with the Lord'. The great East window of Sheffield Cathedral commemorates him.

The hymn which I write of was composed in 1819 at the special request of Edward Bickersteth, a prominent early Evangelical, father of Bishop Bickersteth of Exeter and an ancestor of a great clerical family, one of whom (John Bickersteth) has recently become Bishop of Warrington. Bickersteth had written a treatise on Prayer, and Montgomery's verses were printed in the volume. They make up a commentary on prayer and its meaning that I often find myself wanting to quote.

The inner nature of prayer is brought out in the first two stanzas.

> Prayer is the soul's sincere desire
> Uttered or unexpressed;
> The motion of a hidden fire
> That trembles in the breast.
> Prayer is the burden of a sigh,
> The falling of a tear,
> The upward glancing of an eye
> When none but God is near.

He understands that prayer often conveys thoughts that lie too deep for words, if not for tears. The very desire of the heart, if directed towards God, is itself prayer.

The wide range of prayer is expressed in the contrasts of the next verse:

> Prayer is the simplest form of speech
> That infant lips can try;
> Prayer the sublimest strains that reach
> The Majesty on high.

Prayer as penitence is emphasised in the dramatic picture of the next stanza—perhaps a little too dramatic for the pedestrian levels of modern devotion.

> Prayer is the contrite sinner's voice,
>   Returning from his ways,
> While angels in their songs rejoice,
>   And cry, 'Behold he prays!'

Then come two splendid lines, which could be quoted more often, apart from their being linked with thoughts of death, which are not always in keeping, especially when preaching to the young, as every Bishop does in Confirmation Services.

> Prayer is the Christian's vital breath,
>   The Christian's native air,
> His watchword at the gates of death,
>   He enters heaven with prayer.

The next verse carries deep undertones of some of the more profound teaching of the New Testament about prayer and is much influenced by Our Lord's great High Priestly prayer in St. John 17.

> The saints in prayer appear as one,
>   In word, and deed and mind,
> While with the Father and the Son
>   Sweet fellowship they find.

Compare here, also, I John 1. 3.

So to the last verse, which brings our prayer into a close relationship with the prayer of Our Lord:

> O thou by whom we come to God,
>   The Life, the Truth, the Way,
> The path of prayer thyself hast trod:
>   Lord, teach us how to pray.

'The path of prayer'. Every Christian is called to embark on this path. It would be impossible, within the proportions of this book to describe in detail where that path leads, and what obstacles are likely to impede the pilgrim's progress along it. Perhaps however it may be helpful to look at one or two of the problems that arise in the mind of modern man when he thinks about prayer, or tries to engage in it. One difficulty which may oppress some would-be 'pray-ers' is that of the immense vastness of the universe, and the daring impertinence which may be involved in thinking that one can in any sense 'converse' with the Author and Creator of it all. It involves believing that the thoughts, fears, and hopes of creatures physically as insignificant as midges in the summer air are of interest to, and are heard by the Divine Majesty which sustains the stars in their courses. It is well to face this difficulty squarely, for otherwise it may nag away at the 'sub' or 'semi' conscious levels with disastrous results.

There are no easy answers to great questions of this sort but one can at least set them in their proper place, and see them in their proper proportion. Even in our ordinary human experience, there is virtually no connection between 'size' and 'consciousness'. I say 'virtually' for of course there *is* a difference between what goes on in the mind of a human being and what goes on in the mind of a gnat. But there is no reason to think that when the brain gets larger still (e.g. in an elephant) the quality of consciousness continues to enlarge with it. Consider too the way in which two people deeply in love, or lovingly united (e.g. mother and child) are in close accord and 'empathy' even when separated by many miles of distance. I hesitate to bring in the evidence which television and radar may offer, but one could say just this: if our forefathers could have been told of the moment-by-moment contact preserved between the moon-travellers and the earth they would have regarded it as at least as 'impossible' as some sceptics find prayer to be. Then of course one must remember that we are talking not about converse with a distant 'human being' subject to our limitations. The most radical sceptic would have to agree that 'if there is a God' he could, should he so desire, hear and answer prayer.

If we want to go further than this, and say 'what evidence is there that he does?' we can only fall back on the convictions of all those who have believed in prayer, including of course any convictions that we ourselves have come to hold during the course of our lives, long or short. Prominent, indeed dominant, in such evidence, will be the experience, the example, and the teaching of Our Lord himself. Whatever may be uncertain about the facts of Our Lord's earthly life he is clearly presented to us in all the Gospels as a man of prayer. He was born into a nation with a developed tradition of prayer. The Psalms, which still inspire the prayers of many Christians, were the cradle in which his life of prayer was nurtured. He prayed both with others (in the synagogue) and alone (on the hillside, or in the Garden of Gethsemane). The first, last, and central 'words' on the Cross are prayers. His prayer-life called out from his disciples the request 'Teach us to pray'. A central element in the post-Easter Christian experience was to share his address to the Father, and to use the very same word, 'Abba', that he had been known to use (Galatians 4. 6 and Romans 8. 15).

At the heart of the tradition was the form of prayer which he is said to have given to his disciples—what we know as 'The Lord's Prayer' (St. Matthew 6. 9–13 and St. Luke 11. 2–4). It may be that even in the forms familiar to us the prayer has already been the subject of some 'expansion' through regular use in Christian assemblies or in private devotion. But when allowance has been made for this, we still have a clear picture of prayer as a trustful, reverent, obedient, dependent approach of child to Father.

That is Christ's legacy to us, and for many that will be a sufficient guarantee on which to base their own prayers. To pray in this spirit, and often in these words, is to pray 'in Christ's name'—as he would have us pray, even, we may say, as he would pray in us and through us.

But so great are the problems raised in some Christian's minds about prayer, especially about prayer for things and for people, petitionary and intercessory prayer, that something more must yet be said. Most people can accept without too much difficulty the value of prayer as meditation or reflection. 'To see life steadily and see it whole' is always helpful, and in busy days this calls for withdrawal from the rush of life, and for conscious concentration on the highest and the best that we know. The real difficulty begins when we begin to pray that something may happen, that a sick relative may recover, a heart be changed and softened, a need in God's work met, either by the emergence of a right person for a task, or by the offering of the needed financial resources. Winston Churchill once said—I think it was on the night that Russia was brought into the war—'there are times when all pray'. It is easy to be superior and critical about prayers which are so readily made in crises, and so easily omitted in smoother times, but I do not believe in giving way to this complacent criticism. A sense of need is far from being the *principal* point of contact between man and God but it is commonly the *initial* point of contact, and God certainly uses troubles —I could not say *sends* troubles—to bring people nearer to himself.

But when the prayers begin to rise—either regularly or spasmodically—does anything happen? That is the question. Humanist sceptics say 'no'. Christian believers may often hesitate to say 'yes'. After a long experience I have seen many sad things happen—young lives dashed away in accidents, families bereft through the inexorable advance of incurable disease. These have happened in prayerful families just as frequently—or so it seems to me —as in godless or indifferent homes. Vast natural catastrophes take place in spite of the daily prayer of millions 'Thy Will be done'. Such facts must be squarely faced, or one is living in a world of fantasy and romance.

In other words there is no *guarantee* that prayers however earnest, however trustful, however submissive, will achieve the results which to our human minds seem eminently desirable, and as far as we can tell, in line with the Will of God. And yet most Christians will be ready to say two things.

One is that many blessings that have been received have come to us after long and trustful prayer. For many years now I have kept a prayer notebook with two columns for each month—one headed 'prayer', one headed 'praise'. I just state that it has been a steady encouragement to see how one can frequently transfer an item—an unsolved problem, a critical illness—from the 'prayer' column to the 'praise' column. Even here one must be on one's guard against self-deception and romanticising. Perhaps some of the matters would have settled themselves anyhow by 'the silent lapse of time'. But life can be judged only by the one who is living it, and my view right or wrong, is that prayer *has* influenced many events that otherwise would have remained worrying and frustrating, not harmonised with, or woven into a pattern of peace, and joy and love.

The other thing Christians will say is this. Even when sadness and disaster have ensued, they have not been the same kind of sadness or disaster that they would have been without prayer. I have seen so many women, for instance, called on to accompany their husbands to the edge of the valley of the shadow of death, at which they have to say 'goodbye', and seen them given a strength, perseverance and courage that I cannot describe as other than the result of supernatural grace. To see the bereaved bravely and confidently singing the funeral hymns, to see them concerned not for themselves, but only for others, is to see a glimpse of 'the peace that passeth understanding' and of the joy that no man can take from us.

Of those who have thought deeply and written helpfully about prayer George Macdonald, the nineteenth century Scottish novelist and theologian stands out above most. He faces the difficulty with which this section began, the apparent insignificance of man in the great universe. 'How should any design of the All-wise be altered in response to prayer of ours? How are we to believe such a thing?'—so he asks in 'Man's Difficulty concerning Prayer' (quoted in C. S. Lewis's selections from George Macdonald, Bles, 1946, p. 53). 'Does God care for suns and planets and satellites, for divine mathematics (so Macdonald continues) more than for his children? I venture to say he cares more for oxen than for those. He lays no plans irrespective of his children; and, his design being that they shall be free, active, live things, He sees that space shall be kept for them.' Or again: 'What stupidity of perfection would that be which left no room for change of plan upon change of fact—yea, even the mighty change that . . . now at length his child is praying.' (op. cit., pp. 54–5).

All this is very relevant to the theme 'Life eternal here and hereafter' for prayer is one of the chief ways in which man has fellowship with God. We certainly need not feel that it is only religious activity that prepares us for heaven, but if we believe that to know God is eternal life, we may surmise that the path of prayer is a principal, dare

I say, *the* principal way to a saving, life-giving knowledge of God. It is one side of our lives that nothing *need* take away from us, except complete infirmity of mind, and even then we cannot say whether God has not ways of keeping open channels of communication which we cannot understand. Every clergyman can recall incidents when patients have been apparently in a deep coma, and when they have suddenly responded with a clear 'amen', or other reply to a prayer which the priest thought was far out of the reach of their apparently unconscious mind.

HEARING GOD'S WORD

It is always an interesting question whether to include 'Bible reading' within 'prayer' or whether to consider it as a separate function of the spiritual life. The question is purely technical. All will agree that listening to, reading, or meditating on the words of the Bible has been for countless Christians all down the ages a very important way of growing in grace and in the knowledge of God. It is not necessary to draw too sharp a line between the hearing of Scripture in church and the reading of Scripture in private. For many centuries of Church history only the first was possible, because few could read, and if they could, manuscripts were indescribably scarce. Ordinary Christians in those centuries had to rely on hearing 'the Gospel' read, and possibly translated into the vernacular and briefly explained. Robert Grosseteste would not institute a certain priest to Cossington (now in my diocese) until he had learned the English homilies on the Gospels for each Sunday. But with the coming of printing, and later the extension of education and literacy, it has been possible for many lay Christians to read the Bible for themselves. In some generations this has meant the reading at home of some epistle or gospel previously read, or later to be read, in church. Those who were prevented by work, age or sickness often treated this as a duty. Schemes of personal Bible reading such as those sponsored by the Scripture Union or the Bible Reading Fellowship, have nurtured thousands of Christians during the last fifty years and more. In quite recent times group Bible study has become more popular, and some who could no longer 'get down' to regular Bible reading day by day found here a new way of listening to God's Word as it is conveyed through the written words of prophet, psalmist, evangelist and apostle.

The ways of reading the Bible are legion. One can look at it with a telescope, or with a microscope. By this I mean that it can be looked at in wide stretches—when one surveys long sweeps of Biblical history, as, e.g. the history of Israel, the life of a prophet, the story of Jesus, or of the early Church in Acts. Or one can take the microscope and examine a verse or a phrase in detail. The little phrase 'in Christ', so common in St. Paul, would provide a life time of meditation and study for someone who really wanted to know what it is to be 'in Christ'. Some scholars, such as Adolf Deissmann and Armitage Robinson, have indeed given years of their life to such detailed study.

In some way or another, mature Christians will want and need to be nourished by the Word of God. Man shall not live by bread alone, said Jesus, but by every word that proceedeth out of the mouth of God. The exact relation between the words of the Bible and the Word of God is not easy to describe precisely, but that there is such a relation would be conceded by every Christian who has shown any interest in the subject.

Germanus of Paris, writing in the sixth century (Epistles, I) said this: 'The prophetic lesson keeps its own place, reproving evil things and declaring the future, that we may know Him to be the same God who has thundered in the prophecy, taught in the apostle, and shone forth in the brightness of the Gospel.' With such a key in our minds we can turn to almost any part of the Bible, and find our minds and hearts enriched and refreshed from the sweet springs from which our Church's life took its origin. In the Old Testament we learn of all that Jesus took for granted before his mission began—of God's work in creation, in history, and in revelation. We read the Psalms which he read, and which formed the basis, humanly speaking of his piety and filial trust and obedience. In the Gospels, we are in direct touch with the Word made flesh. We hear his words, and watch his deeds. In the Epistles we listen to the Apostles. We learn how those thought and felt who knew the first impact of the Resurrection, and what it taught them about the significance of the death and passion of Christ. We see them working out the implication of it all—deciding on language to express the relation of God the Son to God the Father, and exploring the endless ethical consequences to be drawn from union with the self-giving of Christ. They discovered, and sketched out for us, what it means to have that mind which was also in Christ Jesus. They found that this had implications at every level—for parents, for children, for employers and employees, for rulers and ruled, for pastors and teachers, and for those whose place it was to be shepherded or taught.

God's messages did not come to a dead stop with the closing of the Canon of Scripture. He spoke, and still speaks, through his saints and his ministers. But the historical nature of our faith causes us to attach special importance to those documents which record the origin and uprising of our faith. Some in every church should be active Bible readers and Bible students. Such are the articulate leaders in the congregation. Such are the ones whose eyes light up as the preacher expounds God's message in its modern and contemporary importance. To share such inspiration is an important part of the *communio in sacris*, the sharing of holy things. The Holy Spirit, we say, 'spake by the prophets'. He also spoke through the Incarnate Christ, and he speaks by those who wrote about him, and about what it means to live by him and through him. 'The flesh profiteth nothing', says Our Lord in St. John 6, 'It is the Spirit that quickeneth. The words that I speak unto you, they are spirit, and they are life.' When at the Communion I say 'Almighty God . . . have mercy upon you . . . and keep you in life eternal', I expect that one way in which he will do this is to feed the people with his Word, written in the Bible, preached from the pulpit, pondered and treasured in the heart.

7

LIFE ETERNAL—
Here and Hereafter (2)

WE HAVE considered one of the principal elements in 'the new life', the life that we believe anticipates, shares in, 'the life of the world to come'. That element was prayer. We saw that prayer extends over a wide field of experience, and includes, or must always be bracketed with, attention to what God is saying to us here and now, through the medium of the Scriptures. But there are various other elements that must be glanced at.

FELLOWSHIP
'In so far as I have any share in the life of the kingdom of God', said Charles Raven, 'it is because my friends have held me there.' He was touching on a subject which has wide repercussions—the place of fellowship with others in 'the new life'. Sometimes I think the importance of the corporate side of religion cannot be overrated. We have moved far from the days when A. N. Whitehead said, 'Religion is what man does with his solitariness.' The New Testament might have warned us not to go too far, or too hastily, along that road. 'Where two or three are gathered together in my name', said Jesus, 'there am I in the midst.' Why was it necessary for the two or three to gather together before they could claim that particular promise? We do not know, but we can guess that a man, a person, becomes more of a man, more of a person, when he is in relationship, especially harmonious relationship with

others. To such a man, in such a relationship, Christ can more easily reveal himself than to a man cut off in isolation. This cannot mean that God has not his own ways of helping the lonely, the solitary, but the special promise is to Christians in fellowship, in company. Experience supports this.

In worship, Christians are linked with previous generations, as they use the same psalms, prayers and hymns as those who have gone before. They may consciously recall the participation of 'the choir invisible' as Anglicans do at the Sanctus: 'Therefore with angels and archangels and with all the company of heaven, we laud and magnify Thy Holy Name . . . ' The use of material well known to all, or nearly all participants, has a liberating and uniting effect. To take an obvious example, a congregation meeting on Easter morning, and being invited to sing 'Jesus Christ is risen today' is immediately bound together as it takes on its lips words well-known and well-adapted to express their corporate hopes and praises.

Alongside the liturgical fellowship there is a place and a call for much social and personal fellowship. Indeed a long experience in the ministry makes me almost ready to say that no spiritual fellowship will last long unless it leads to, and is supported by, many opportunities to meet as friends, and as sharers in practical enterprises for the church, for the neighbourhood, or those in special need. In these matters we have learned a lot from the Church in the United States. There it is the regular custom for those who have been together in Eucharistic worship to adjourn for coffee and talk. This custom has spread to very many English parishes holding Parish Communions, and it is of very great importance. It is not just a matter of adding a pleasant half-hour of chat to a formal service: it is rather a matter of giving the Eucharistic fellowship some positive content in the sphere of personal relationships. It is at least an interesting coincidence, to put it no higher than that, that when Pliny wrote to Trajan describing Christian customs in Asia about A.D. 113 he mentioned that after their early morning sacramental occasion the Christians met again 'for ordinary and harmless food'. This has usually been taken to imply some kind of lovefeast or *agape*, and it is something very similar that is involved today. Needless to say the life of the fellowship is a very much more complex thing than the provision of minor social occasions. It involves all the mutual interlocking of lives and of families that a Christian congregation both demands and very often supplies. Perhaps all this comes to life most obviously when the joy or sorrow of one family is obviously shared by others, but this can only happen in a significant way if there is 'normal-level' fellowship to act as a 'carrier' for the 'deep-level' fellowship that is occasionally required.

It was Charles Wesley who wrote so clearly about Eucharistic fellowship as a foretaste of heaven. The hymn which most clearly expresses it is not an example of his finest poetry, but it was deemed worthy of being included in *Hymns Ancient and Modern Revised* (No. 420).

> How glorious is the life above
> > Which in this ordinance we taste,
> That fulness of celestial love,
> > That joy which shall for ever last!

The last verse strikes the same note.

> Sure pledge of ecstacies unknown
> > Shall this divine Communion be:
> The ray shall rise into a sun,
> > The drop shall swell into a sea.

It is impossible to say what particular train of thought led Charles Wesley to see in the Holy Communion an anticipation of the fellowship and worship of heaven. An eschatological note is of course struck in the Consecration prayer, with the words 'until his coming again', which echo I Corinthians 11. 26, 'Ye do shew forth his death till he come'. But it is more likely that the deep experiences of joy and adoration which he received in the Communion struck him as having the texture of eternity. He was experiencing 'Life eternal', and looked for its continuance in the life of the world to come.

SERVICE AND SACRIFICE

'Send us out into the world, in the power of the Spirit, to live and work to thy praise and glory.' These words, from the deservedly popular short prayer of dedication which concludes the Series II Communion Service, summarise another aspect of 'life eternal here'—it is a life of sacrificial service. This is clearly taught in the New Testament. 'By love serve one another.' 'Bear ye one another's burdens.' 'We that are strong ought to bear the infirmities of them that are weak.' 'Love your neighbour as yourself' —there is no shortage of crisp quotations. The same teaching is prominent in the Gospels, where the parables of the Good Samaritan and the Sheep and the Goats give unmistakable calls to a spirit of love and care for those in every kind of need, physical, social or emotional. All down the ages this spirit of service has found expression in social and personal service of various kinds. The record of the Church is by no means uniform. It includes many episodes that we should like to forget—imperial domination under Byzantine Emperors, gross luxury and license under the Borgia popes, inquisitorial torture, the slaughter of ecclesiastical rivals (Protestants by Catholics and Catholics by Protestants), the well-meaning but often insensitive paternalism of Victorian clergy—the list could be extended interminably. But alongside all this there is an equally long list of social ventures and initiatives—care for slaves under the semi-christianised Constantine, hostels for beggars and lepers in the Middle Ages, the Franciscan movement seeking Christ in his poor, Victorian philanthropy and social challenge, bringing education to the people, care for orphans, the blind and the deaf, the first steps in labour regulation (the Ten-Hours-Parson was the name given to a clergyman who led the case for the reduction of labour to a maximum of ten hours a day). In modern times the zeal of Christians with strong social sympathies has moved on to the needs of the Third World, and to vigorous campaigning on behalf of those handicapped by colour and race in the complex society of the modern world.

A proper sense of commitment to those in any kind of need is undoubtedly a part of commitment to Christ in any age, and in the modern age it calls for public action (sometimes political action) perhaps more clearly than for service at a more personal level, some of which will undoubtedly be rendered in any case by the representatives of an ever-more efficient 'health and welfare service'. But every one is different—possibilities vary enormously, so do temperaments, so do resources of time and money. A member of Parliament will have responsibilities differing from those of, shall we say, a pensioned-off industrial worker, the wife of an agricultural labourer, or a grammar-school teenager. But there is a thread of common obligation running through the lives of all committed Christian people. It is difficult to define—perhaps one could say that it is an obligation to approach nearer and nearer to the character so well described in I Corinthians 13. There we see how St. Paul described the one characteristic which is basic to Christian character, love or 'charity'. Whatever else this means, it means a willingness, no, a desire, to put self second, and others first. This is the root of the courtesy, consideration and compassion which is the undoubted hallmark of the Christ-controlled and Christ-constrained life.

Every one must work out for himself what this means in daily life. One can apply to it the words in the Bible 'It is the spirit that quickeneth: the flesh profiteth nothing'. Nothing is to be gained by a detailed, legalistic prescription of what may be required. If the spirit is right, the actions will be right. But there is something to be said which is of particular relevance to the link between life eternal here and life eternal hereafter. It is this. At the very heart of all characteristic Christianity stands the Cross, but the Christian Cross speaks of both death and resurrection, sacrifice and conquest, defeat and victory. It is the steady experience of Christians that in a measure they share this two-fold fellowship with their Master. Nowhere is it described more forcefully than in 2 Corinthians 12 and 13. 'Most gladly . . . will I . . . glory in my weaknesses, that the power of Christ may rest upon me. Wherefore I take pleasure in weaknesses, in injuries, in necessities, in persecutions, in distresses, for Christ's sake: when I am weak, then am I strong.' Or again: 'He was crucified through weakness, yet he liveth through the power of God. For we also are weak in him, but we shall live with him through the power of God toward you.' All this means that our service for others involves a rejection of the world's weapons of force, domination, and threats, and an acceptance of Christ's weapons of love, understanding, and service. This may involve actual losses, of money, prestige, and power. It is not a policy one can impose on others (e.g. the State) but it is a principle one can adopt for oneself, and in a measure for the Church. And those who have tried to put it into practice will testify that again and again sacrifices made for the sake of Christ, as he comes before us in the sick, the poor, the anxious, the bereaved, or down-trodden are transformed into victories of varying kind and degree. One just knows that the labour and the effort has *not* been in vain. Sometimes one is rewarded here and now with an obvious triumph for God's cause, a home reconciled, a mourner comforted and uplifted, health restored, a soul won for Christ. Sometimes there is nothing immediate to show—only a sense that one has shouldered some infinitesimal share of 'the afflictions of Christ', filling up some tiny part of that burden which he and his share together. If so, one knows that 'if we suffer with him, we shall also be glorified together'. This double experience, the suffering and the conquering, is very central to true Christian commitment. Many share in it who are quite inarticulate and non-theological—who would never think of describing it in these terms. Many share it, or so I would believe, who do not consciously follow Christ or seek to do his will. But whether they know it or not, they are qualifying for the Lord's commendation 'Inasmuch as ye did it unto one of the least of these my brethren, ye did it unto me.'

> Where'er the gentle heart
>   Finds courage from above;
> Where'er the heart forsook
>   Warms with the breath of love;
> Where faith bids fear depart,
> City of God, thou art.

And this sense of living by the rules of the City of God is a wonderful anticipation of Heaven. There, the Lamb is in the midst of the Throne—at the heart of Rule is Love. And that love, and its victory over evil, in us and in others, is perhaps the most important link between 'life eternal here' and 'life eternal hereafter'.

DISCIPLINE

Few words are so unpopular as the word 'discipline'. The discipline of the child, though still regarded as in some way necessary in the very early stages of life, is frequently put in contrast to that freedom for self-development which is certainly a feature necessary to the environment of those growing into maturity. Discipline at school is a subject of sharp and sometimes bitter controversy. Most enlightened teachers seem to do well enough without the use of corporal punishment, and the stress is on free activity, allowing the child to do what he likes when he likes, rather than putting him through a pre-arranged time-table in which he passively takes in what is put before him. Social attitudes have made the task of parents very difficult if they attempt to control the behaviour and time-table of their teenage children. Some achieve a good deal through very tactful, loving influence. Others give up the attempt, feeling that they cannot bear the strain of that emotional separation from their children which so easily follows an attempt to impose upon them restraints which their contemporary friends do not have to undergo. At the University the position has altered since the age of majority has been reduced to 18, for the undergraduates are no longer *in statu pupillari* in relation to parents or the state. 'Discipline' in the accepted use of the word ought not to be necessary at their stage but experience shows that many of the accepted objects of University life are maintained only with great difficulty when the student body assumes an attitude to the authorities of the University similar to that of militant strikers to an unpopular management. Even self-discipline, which might easily be thought of as the acceptable substitute for most forms of imposed discipline, is under fire.

Exponents of a permissive morality are quick to point out that 'the acceptance of oneself' is a necessary accompaniment of acceptance by God, and it is not always clear whether this means acceptance of oneself as one is, or the acceptance of oneself as in need of God's help and forgiveness. 'Just as I am' is an excellent attitude to take when throwing onself on God's unlimited love and mercy. It is not equally satisfactory if taken as the highest goal to aim at, especially at a time in life when character, habits, relationships, and even health are at their most exposed and impressionable stage.

Discipline in Christian life is not given much emphasis. No doubt many of the ways in which it was previously taught and practised are necessarily out of date. One sees, however, that with the rapid development of Parish Communion in mid-morning or in the evening, the old disciplines of early rising, fasting, and devotional preparation are gone. I am far from thinking that the exchange is necessarily a bad one, but its existence must be recognised. In theological colleges the idea of expecting students to be regular at Chapel is almost outmoded. Nothing but a spontaneous desire to attend is recognised as of value, and not all teachers or students feel that even this is desirable. The use of forms of service which do not meet the immediate wishes of those taking part or arise from their suggestions, is much criticised, and in fact, rarely attempted. Older restrictions on the use of Sunday, fixed habits of prayer and Bible reading, discipline in language, even in personal relationships, heterosexual or homosexual, are all treated as expendable—not all of them, all the time, but some of them, some of the time, in many influential circles of theological thought and writing.

Errors made in the past have doubtless contributed to this state of affairs. It is always easier to say 'Thou shalt not', and to give a clear content to the prohibition, than to say 'Thou shalt' and to give a clear content to the exhortation. The importance of spontaneity and freedom should never have been overlooked in a religion which claimed to offer men 'the glorious liberty of the children of God'. It is always wrong to suggest that sexual sins are the only ones. Indeed the teaching of Our Lord lays special stress on the possibility of forgiveness of them and of deliverance from them. Christ came that we might have life, and have it more abundantly.

But is there not another side? Certainly nothing in the New Testament suggests that the moral struggle is easy, or still less, unimportant. St. Paul tells us that he buffeted his own body, to bring it into subjection, lest having preached to others, he himself should be a castaway. The race is long and hard; perseverance and patience are required. Those who endure to the end are to be saved. Straight is the gate, and narrow is the way, and few there be that find it. These are all authentic New Testament notes. They find expression, among other places, in the 'household codes' which conclude many of the Epistles. Fathers, children, husbands, wives, masters, servants, are all shown the appropriate ways in which they must show their Christian principles in their particular situations. Of course the actual expressions used are influenced by the social and domestic conditions of the first century in the Eastern Mediterranean world. It would be a miracle if they exactly fitted our modern world. But the wonderful thing is how little adaptation they do need. 'Consideration for others' is the underlying principle; fathers for children, children for fathers, husbands for wives, wives for husbands. And far from suggesting that sexual aberrations are unimportant, St. Paul says that they are particularly dangerous. 'Flee fornication. Every sin that a man doeth is without the body; but he that committeth fornication sinneth against his own body.' (I Corinthians 6. 18). Or, as the N.E.B. expresses it, 'Shun fornication. Every other sin that a man can commit is outside the body; but the fornicator sins against his own body.' Sexual actions and attitudes involve the whole personality.

Every experienced pastor knows that 'there is something' in this. Sexual sin (e.g. adultery after marriage) may not be worse in God's sight than selfishness within it, but it sets repercussions in action which are incredibly difficult to deal with. The husband or the wife who has become involved with another woman or man respectively has set up another mind, another will, which has a vested interest in maintaining the irregular liaison. Every priest knows that it is the hardest job in the world to detach two such people from each other. The *best* side of the erring partner may feel unable to desert the third party, just because that party has become particularly vulnerable through his or her action, especially if already married to another spouse. The doctrine that 'a triangular relationship' could be helpful to all three, as set out in a Quaker pamphlet on sex some years ago, does not accord with my pastoral experience.

So, unpopular though the idea may be, I believe that 'life eternal here' is something more than a riot of self-expression, something more than a ruthless pursuance of social and international ends which in themselves may deserve full support—it includes an element of discipline, of holding fast to that which is good, and of continually renouncing evil. Far from being relevant only to childhood and adolescence, it is a call to life-long vigilance. 'Let him that thinketh he standeth take heed lest he fall.'

But no one need think that the rejection of evil is an impoverishment of life. Only those who are not the servants of sin are free to be free indeed.

HEREAFTER

We must now give some attention to what most people mean by 'life eternal' viz. life for ever after death. It need hardly be said that like most of the basic Christian doctrines, this too has been much questioned in recent years. Opinion polls produce frightening figures in which it is said that large numbers even of regular church-attenders do not believe in life beyond the grave. Some clergymen take an agnostic view of the matter, and radical theologians are inclined to say—in fact actually do say—that those who are fully engaged in the exciting tasks of life here need not spend time thinking about a life beyond this. It is clearly a matter to which any up-to-date appraisal of Christian faith must give attention.

Ever since the writings of the late Dr. O. C. Quick it has been a commonplace to stress the wide divergencies between Christian ideas of resurrection from the dead and Greek ideas of the immortality of the soul. That there is such a wide divergence cannot be denied, and later we shall need to look at it, and to discern its true character. But before we do so, it will be profitable to see how daring was the Greek conception, and to note at least some matters in which the Greek and the Christian attitudes run side by side.

For a typical picture of the Greek viewpoint, we can examine Plato's dialogue, *Phaedo*. This claims to describe events during the last day of the life of Socrates, when he was preparing to drink the hemlock. That event took place in 399 B.C., and the dialogue must be dated after that—how long no one can say. Perhaps it was written about 390 B.C.

Let me briefly describe the contents of this remarkable dialogue—it will be familiar to some of my readers but not to all. One of Socrates' former friends, Echecrates, asks Phaedo, who was present in the prison on Socrates' last day of life, how the great man died, and what he said during that last day. This gives Phaedo an opportunity to describe the whole conversation. The general picture is that his friends are very sad, but that he is quietly content. This fact leads to a number of questions being asked about the immortality of the soul, and in the course of the debate both the arguments against immortality are brought out (by his friends) and the rational basis for Socrates' faith in the life beyond explained. The sceptical view is well expressed by Cebes. 'In what concerns the soul', he says, 'men are apt to be incredulous; they fear that when she has left the body, her place may be nowhere, and that on the very day of death she may perish and come to an end—immediately on her release from the body issuing forth dispersed like smoke or air and in her flight vanishing away into nothingness . . . Surely it requires a great deal of argument and many proofs, to show that when the man is dead, his soul yet exists, and has any force or intelligence.' (Works of Plato: Jowett's Translation, Vol. II. p. 209.) This is very much like the fear that many modern people, including Christian people, have to fight against. Another way in which the difficulty is put is that the harmony which sounds forth from a lyre is something that partakes of eternal beauty, but when the lyre is smashed and broken, where is the harmony? Is not the soul similar? asks one of the company. The modern reader, taught by biologists to believe that consciousness is a function of material organisms, is tempted to feel the same difficulty.

To these, and other questions, Socrates answers with a serene faith. Some of the *mythology* with which he expresses his faith is quaint and eccentric. He believes, for instance, that if a soul has been clearly in bondage to bodily desires it will prove unfit for any better fate than to enter into animals, and those not the most exalted. Even those who have shown only social and political virtues may have to be content with inhabiting 'social' animal communities like those of the bees or wasps! But those who have been devoted to *philosophy*, to the quest for true, undistorted knowledge of the real, may look forward to congenial company in the bodiless life. The sphere of this life is described in the later part of the Phaedo. It is full of fantastic features, but its final passage bears marked similarities to the descriptions of heaven in Revelation—some of the very same precious stones being used in both books to describe the beauties of the abode of the blessed.

Now there are many features in Plato's picture far removed from those of the Bible and the Church. There is, for instance, no place of any kind for the body in Plato's eternal world, only for a liberated soul. Christianity pays at least lip-service to a 'resurrection of the body'. The impurity to be left behind in Plato is not that of sin, but of ignorance and delusion. The whole idea of re-incarnation is not acceptable to Christians. But there are certain points where Plato's testimony is to be welcomed. However he describes his faith, he believes that man is more than just the psychosomatic unit that we believe animals to be. Something about him links him to an eternal world, a world above the change and decay of daily life here on earth. The peace and even joy with which Socrates approaches the moment of death bears a marked similarity to the words which St. Paul uses in Philippians about having 'a desire to depart and to be with Christ, which is very far better'. Whatever differences there are between Plato and St. Paul there are some marked affinities.

One point in particular must be mentioned. The idea of 'the resurrection of the body' as previously understood, included the idea of an actual reconstituting of the body laid in the grave. The metaphor of sleeping and waking lent itself to such naïve conceptions. Many of the older hymns moved in the same circle of ideas, especially

> On the resurrection morning
> Soul and body meet again.

Now however many orthodox Christian theologians insist that they are 'resurrection men' and not 'immortality men'—Hebrew in thought, not Greek—I am quite certain that in their hearts they think of 'the soul' as detached from the body in death, and leave that soul trustfully 'in the hands of God'. They may believe, as I do, that 'God giveth it a body as it hath pleased him', that life eternal is a fuller, not a more shadowy existence than life here. In that sense we may still believe in 'the resurrection of the body'. However, having officiated at countless funerals and cremations, I feel I must testify to my belief that the soul (or spirit) has its own future destiny, and that this can be thought of, as Plato thought of it, as having its own future, having left the body behind.

There is, of course, one mighty difference between all pre-Christian or non-Christian ideas, and the basic foundation of Christian belief in 'the life of the world to come'. This is that we believe that it is *in Christ* that our hope of resurrection lies. 'As in Adam all die, even so in Christ shall all be made alive'. 'I am the resurrection and the life', says Our Lord. The whole story of the Christian Church begins on this side of Easter. It is only because of what happened on Easter Day and afterwards that any

118

one was interested to collect information on what had gone before. Ever since the first Easter Day, the Christian Church has gathered round a Christ who 'was dead and is alive again'. 'Because He lives, we shall live also.'

Belief in the after-life cannot be taken on 'from cold', to use a motoring metaphor. Looked at from a merely scientific point of view, there is little to show that human beings have a life when their body is dead. Their lives may have been beautiful while they lasted, but so is the life of a daffodil or a rose. When the flower fades that is the end of *that* flower. Others may come next year. Memories may last a long time. The passing beauty of the flower may partake of an eternal beauty, whether or not that eternal beauty has any existence other than in the mind. Where are we to find firm ground for the life beyond the grave?

Primarily, as we have said, in our fellowship with the risen Christ. But we need a few supporting props for our faith, which is never strong enough to withstand all doubts.

We may as well admit that apart from the faith we have in the risen Christ there is no *proof* that life survives death. If we believe it, we believe it because of faith, not because of sight. But that faith need not be a foolish, or irrational faith. It ought to stand up to clear and calm examination.

We might begin by noting the marvellous powers of the human consciousness. Not only does this open the way for a Plato, a Dante, a Michael Angelo, or a Beethoven, and all the thousands of lesser intelligences that we know of or can imagine, but even ordinary folk have 'inside them' an instrument compared with which the most sophisticated computer is like a clumsy, pre-historic cart or plough. The most ordinary mind is capable of surveying the stars, remembering past ages, contemplating the future, enjoying the sun, falling in love. All this can be brought to a dead stop, in its present form, by intoxicating the brain, or by a cerebral disaster, but the thought must arise as to whether by that time the soul, the personality, has not achieved some existence independent of the tissues which have previously 'carried' it. Nature provides some illustrations of similar transmutations (e.g. the butterfly and the chrysalis) but we have no grounds on which we can claim them as real parallels.

Apart from revelation, one must just decide for oneself whether the extinction of one's friends and relatives is really thinkable. Of course we have such anxious reasons for hoping that it is not that our reason may be hopelessly biased, and we must make allowance for this. I remember when my father was dying he said to me 'I think the end is near'. I found myself curiously tongue-tied and stumbled out something like this: 'Yes, I think it is but we have had some grand times together haven't we?' 'Wonderful', he replied, 'and it's better further on.' I remember thinking, 'If there were not a future life, God would have to create one, to reward a faith like that.' And such an idea is not fantastic. Our Lord taught that the one ground for faith in the world to come is God himself. 'He is not a God of the dead, but of the living.' Just as in this life, all we are depends on God's continuing act of creation ('God holds us over the abyss', said Karl Barth) so God is capable of extending his creative power into other worlds than this. We can say with sincerity 'I believe in the life of the world to come,' only if we can also say 'I believe in God, in Christ, in the Life-giving Spirit and in the Church.'

Having said that, one can then enjoy to the full the symbolic and poetic clothing which has been given to our Christian hope. I attended the funeral service of Bishop Joost de Blank in Westminster Abbey. At a certain point

the casket containing his ashes was solemnly carried down
to the West End to be deposited. As the choir returned
they burst into Peter Abelard's great hymn.

> Oh what the joy and the glory must be
>   Those endless Sabbaths the blessed ones see,
> Crown for the valiant, to weary ones rest;
>   God shall be All, and in all ever blest.

I find it hard to describe the increasing crescendo of hope
and confidence that spread through the Abbey as verse
after verse of that hymn soared up to the vaulted roof
above. All that Peter Abelard longed for, and knew that
he must wait for, till this life was ended, seemed a living
reality for Joost de Blank as we sang of that Jerusalem
which is 'dear native land' to true Christians. The sceptic
can claim that this is just wishful thinking. The believer
can take the plunge of faith, and say, 'I believe'. He may
have to add 'Help Thou mine unbelief'. If he does, that
prayer will not go unanswered.

One of the well-known couplets in the hymn runs thus:

> Wish and fulfilment can sever'd be ne'er
>   Nor the thing prayed for come short of the prayer.

This is one of the great supports for faith in the world to
come. God has put eternity in our hearts. There is that in
us which can never be satisfied with passing joys and
pleasures. All the poets have written of the pathos of
fleeting beauty.

> Fair daffodils, we weep to see
>   You haste away so soon.

So the human heart fixes its hopes, among the sundry and
manifold changes of the world, where true joys are to be
found.

And in those halls of Sion
All joy shall be complete
For in that land of beauty,
All things of beauty meet.

We just have to decide whether this wonderful faith
has our vote. Browning said:

It may be false, but would you wish it true?
Has it your vote to be so, if it can?

That is faith's venture, and I pray that every reader of
this book may be given strength and courage to take that
plunge of faith.